Aloysius *and Friends*

Donna Fritz; Aunt Gerry Caldwell

authorHOUSE®

AuthorHouse™
1663 Liberty Drive
Bloomington, IN 47403
www.authorhouse.com
Phone: 1 (800) 839-8640

Published by AuthorHouse 05/08/2015

ISBN: 978-1-5049-0706-4 (sc)
ISBN: 978-1-5049-0705-7 (e)

Print information available on the last page.

Any people depicted in stock imagery provided by Thinkstock are models,
and such images are being used for illustrative purposes only.
Certain stock imagery © Thinkstock.

This book is printed on acid-free paper.

for my beloved Aloysius

With special thanks to:
Julie, for the tiny joey who became my soulmate
Aunt Gerry and Louise
Lucille, as always
Persephone and Rhonda,
for making me spit on my keyboard
Drs. Martin and Shing, and the staff of the CVH
Dr. Spindel and the staff at Animal Ark
Glenn and the staff at Lime Hollow
and all opossum fans everywhere.

Prologue *(by Julie Magura)*

Meeting my possum friend Aloysius

So many of our days are about going through the motions. We know what is in front of us, predictable, so we diligently knock out task after task.

Then there are the days where we are derailed into something else entirely, for better or worse. Those are the days where we have chance encounters with grace and magic amidst the unexpected.

The day that I found Aloysius was one of those days. Taking care of my body has been an endless task the past many years. I was driving into my chiropractor's office when teetering in front of me was the tiniest little possum I had ever seen. I nearly hit him. Yikes!

I parked immediately and jumped out of my car, terrified that someone else might not see him as I had. He quickly disappeared under a car in front of mine so I hurried on out. I grabbed the green towel that I had on hand for my neighbor's dog, and asked another woman in the parking lot to stand on one side of the car to block the little possum from running out to the other side.

It wasn't too difficult to nab the little guy. It was quite apparent that he was too exhausted to run off, but then again they are nocturnal creatures. And he was so little! I really didn't know too much about possums other than the fact that when they get overwhelmed they go into a kind of narcoleptic sleep. I've seen that on the farm where I live, when the resident dog has found one in daylight to harrass. I thought for a second about turning him out into the shrubs and brush on the hillside edge of the lot, but that thought very quickly passed out of my mind. It was at that moment I decided I would try and find someone to care for him, becoming my day's mission. Why on earth would he be wandering around a busy parking lot? Was he lost, had his mother met an ill fate? It didn't really matter at that point, he needed someone but I knew most likely I wasn't prepared to be his person.

The woman who helped me in the parking lot had scurried off, looking at me strangely by my insistence on pulling this baby possum out from under a car. Looking back it might have seemed odd, but I've always rooted for the underdog. Possums seem to have gotten a bad rap in the world. And holy moly was this guy soft!

I went into my chiropractor's office with him wrapped in the green towel and proceeded to get my thrice weekly adjustment. They didn't mind one bit that I was walking around with wildlife in my arms setting him down while I lay on the table. Honestly, I couldn't imagine leaving him. I nicknamed him the Sweet Little Sea Urchin because my chiropractor's office is called Sea Change. He seemed like a small street urchin lost in a sea of asphalt.

First I went up to the SPCA where I was supposed to volunteer that afternoon. I was told they don't care for wildlife, and that I should try the Cornell Wildlife Vet clinic. They sent me on my way with a small carrier, some milk replacer and a handful of feeding syringes.

Cornell told me that they couldn't take him, that their wildlife rehabilitator had gone back to work full time and was no longer taking any rescued animals. Uh oh. However, they gave me a small list of phone numbers for some area veterinarians who might know what to do. They also suggested picking up some oranges, grapes and electrolyte replacer. So I headed right into Wegmans with my soft urchin in the carrier and asked if I could leave him at the service desk while I shopped. I couldn't believe it, but they said yes! I was too afraid to leave him alone for even one minute. I then headed home with the possum and fruit in tow.

I called around and left numerous messages. I got two returned calls, one from another shelter about 30 miles west who offered to meet with me later that day, and after that a call from a woman named Donna who seemed extremely knowlegable about possums. Fortunately one of the vets I had left a message with contacted her and she called me about an hour later. She gave me so much information and I learned that possums are the only marsupials in the US, and actually have opposable thumbs. I looked at his tiny little hands, because that's what they were, delicate little hands, not paws.

He ate a few bites of a grape and took a little bit of milk replacer but nothing else. For a while I set him loose on the floor of my bathroom but he didn't seem too thrilled about this. When on the phone with Donna she told me how to check his anatomy, so I figured out he was a boy. Back in the green towel I held him gingerly in my arms waiting until my appointed meeting times.

Donna offered to drive and meet me at a middle point up near the community college later on that day. I felt a bit conflicted. Who should I give him to? Where would he have the best chance of getting better and possibly being released? I felt like I was on a quest. I knew that I had absolutely no idea how to care for a sick little possum, even despite a childhood filled with caring for baby rabbits and birds displaced by the neighborhood cats.

Later that afternoon I met with the other woman who had told me she was already driving into Ithaca from Watkins Glen. She looked over the little guy and pronounced that he was't well at all and although she would take him, things didn't look so good. It also sounded like she was a bit overwhelmed with many other critters in her care, especially since it was a busy clinic. I decided to hold off and meet with Donna. She had me convinced that she absolutely loved possums, had her wildlife license and had had more than a few in her care over the years.

When I met with Donna, she also could see that the little guy needed immediate care and veterinary attention. Ironically she had two more possums on the way that weekend and asked me if perhaps I might consider giving it a go. I was just too nervous and I really wanted him to make it. On top of that I already had a lot of responsibility living on a farm with two cats, five horses and a dog.

I had to trust her, so I passed him off. She was incredibly prepared and promised to do absolutely everything she could.

Thus begins the journey of sweet little Aloysius. I've followed his adventures and received regular updates about his health progress, the unique life and the love and joy he brought into the life of Donna. How cool is that!

Chapter 1

The Sweet Sea Urchin Finds a Home

The baby opossum huddled there on the hot pavement, too weak to move out of the ovenlike late-June sun. No longer did he hope for the security of his mother, the comfort of her rich milk, or the companionship of his siblings. Now he merely hoped to remain unnoticed by the many terrors surrounding him. He was beyond thirst, having descended far into advanced dehydration. Lightheaded and dizzy from severe anemia, he was too enervated to even pull off some of the dozens of ticks that continued to suck the remaining vitality from his tiny body.

Suddenly his worst fear came to life, as a giant two-legged creature cornered him beneath a large, smelly metal thing, then a second creature reached and closed her hands around his trembling form. His painful struggles were ignored, and he was taken away from the sky and outdoors, and everything he had ever known, closed into a plastic crate.

The scary creature made soft sounds that made him feel a bit calmer, and then he was given a succulent, sweet grape!

"You're a sweet sea urchin," the human informed him, as he chewed and swallowed slowly but gratefully.

Over the next several hours – a terribly long time for such a small baby – the ticks relentlessly pulled the lifeblood from his depleted veins. He was barely conscious when his captor-turned-savior took him for a long ride in a vehicle.

A new human picked him up, but the baby possum was beyond caring, beyond the ability to make even a token struggle. He lay unmoving, even when he felt a sharp sting, then another and another, as the vicious ticks were ripped from his tender flesh, including his eyelids and inside his ears. Over one hundred ticks later, the little marsupial finally fell unconscious. He never felt when the fly eggs were similarly plucked, one by one with tweezers, from the abrasion on his left hip.

He awoke when he felt himself immersed in warm water. Somehow he found the energy to panic at the prospect of imminent drowning, but he was held firmly, although gently, with his head kept well above the surface. He inhaled the floral scent of lavender as the woman tenderly lathered his skeletal body, then rinsed him off, several times.

More pain as previously-hidden ticks were discovered, removed, and killed. The possum heard anger in this new caretaker's voice, but by her nearly nonstop smooching he knew her fury was directed at the parasites and not himself. Clean by nature, he felt better after the bath, but utterly exhausted, and he lay inert in the woman's hand as she dried him off and settled him gently into a soft nest.

He slept, but not for very long it seemed, before he was taken to yet another bewildering place. Bright, and loud with the cries of predators large enough to eat him whole and look for more, this place smelled not of soothing flowers, but antiseptic, dogs and cats, and fear.

The woman slid her hands beneath him and brought him out of the relative safety of the fleecy nest in his crate. Kissing him yet again, she set him on a soft blanket on a table, and introduced him to the veterinarian. The quiet, gentle man looked him over, felt his arms and legs, spine and stomach, held an absurdly large stethoscope to his ribs and listened to his starving heart, then peered into his eyes and mouth and ears.

A large needle pierced the skin between his shoulder blades, but the pain was brief, followed by warmth flooding his body as the fluids he had been robbed of for so long were replaced. Another, much smaller, injection gave him some energy, and a third, the vet explained, was an antibiotic because of the ticks. The vet didn't like them any more than the little possum's caretaker did.

Then his human carefully set him back inside the crate, and soon they had returned to the calm house with only one dog, who politely avoided him. The woman took him out again and cuddled him, kissing him, her warm breath ruffling his damp fur.

"Please live, my little love," the woman pleaded softly into the drowsy possum's ear. "My little Aloysius."

His mother was gone, but by a miracle he was once more in the care of someone who loved him. Aloysius drifted off to sleep, clinging tightly to his human's fingers with both hands.

Chapter 2

New Year's Kiss

Aloysius loved the big black exercise wheel, even though it was uncomfortably close to the hot, noisy pellet stove, with it attendant soot that had turned his tail black despite his obsessive cleaning, and the rough ashes under his tender hands and feet that escaped his human's careful sweeping. Plus, even though it was dark outside now in the middle of the night, the flames behind the window of the thing kept this room perpetually bright.

No matter. He was a possum, and took everything in stride, focusing intently on enjoying the good things and easily dismissing the bad. There will always be plenty of either, depending on which you look for.

Aloysius put one hand on the textured walking surface that moved gently beneath his touch, then clumsily hopped up on, scrabbling a bit before he started walking, making enough noise to bring Mom on the run.

"Hey, little love." She knelt down next to the wheel. Aloysius stopped walking as she petted him and kissed the top of his head, her touch so light it didn't disrupt his chronically shaky balance. He really didn't need help walking on the wheel, but it made her feel good to lightly touch his side as he walked, so he didn't mind. He clicked at her, his dextrous hand catching hold of the the fingers petting his face.

The small opossum turned to give her knuckles a quick lick and dragged his head backwards across them, losing his balance as the wheel moved beneath him. Deciding to indulge in a proper lick-rub, Aloysius stepped off the wheel and took hold of the woman's hand once more as she hunched over the top of him, kissing him from shoulders to hips and murmuring how much she loved him.

Applying a generous layer of spit on the back of her hand, Aloysius drew his face across her fingers from jawline to nose, over and over, switching sides periodically, making the fur on the top of his head stand up like a mohawk. Tightly he gripped her fingers in his own strong hand, both to hold her in place and assist his dicey balance. Over and over he lick-rubbed deliriously, with vigor and enthusiasm, as his human continued to hug and smooch him, making happy sounds.

Suddenly, the mantel clock chimed its full melodic song, then announced the hour with deep gongs. Aloysius felt his human suddenly go still as the last gong echoed away.

"Aloysius! You've given me my first ever New Year's kiss! Oh, happy New Year, my love!" With this, she fell into a near-smothering smooch session that even the highly affectionate Aloysius found a trifle overwhelming, but he licked and clicked and continued headrubbing her, as she laughed and cried and kissed him.

She might be a strange human, but she was *his* human, and Aloysius loved her just as she was.

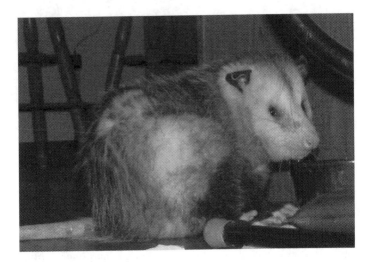

Chapter 3

Bangs and Kibbles

He wasn't exactly hungry, but Aloysius wanted a particular snack, and being a clever opossum, had trained his human to dispense this specific treat at his whim, any time of the day or night (but he usually preferred night.)

Walking with sideways steps up to the placemat where the two stainless-steel dog bowls sat, one full of water and one empty, the six-pound opossum leaned one hand on the edge of the water bowl and drank. His human tried very hard to keep the water clean and fresh, but usually as soon as she rinsed and refilled the bowl, the big sloppy dog had to check it out, leaving the water with a distinct taste of drool, and a layer of slime at the bottom. However, Aloysius didn't feel like hiking across the room to the small bowl of clean water she kept just for him, which the dog was forbidden to touch. He finished and turned his attention to the empty bowl.

Taking the edge of the bowl in one hand, Aloysius pulled it across the floor, tipping it sideways, making a satisfying *bang-crash!* on the wood floor. He waited a few seconds to see if his acolyte had awakened. Nope. She lay silent and still, the tick-tock of the cuckoo clock loud in the quiet.

He essayed another round of banging, and after a minute or two, she sat up, removed the dog from across her legs, and stood groggily. "You want some dog food, little love?" she asked, stumbling sleepily over to peer at him in the dim light of the nightlight, wrapping her robe about her.

Aloysius banged the dish again in answer. He was proud of how smart his human was, how easily trained, and how eagerly she leaped to grant his every wish (or at least the ones he could make clear to her. She was a human, after all, not a marsupial.) He clicked loudly at her, as she petted his sides symmetrically so as not to disrupt his dicey balance.

Finally she pulled open the cupboard door and fished out a small handful of delightfully crunchy kibble from the container, coaxing him away from the door with it so she could shut it without hitting him. Then she knelt by his side and held the food in the palm of her hand while he ate. She preferred he didn't eat off the floor, but Aloysius didn't mind. There were often little tidbits under the birdcage which he cheerfully cleaned up, but he could only do that when she wasn't watching, or she'd stop him, telling him they weren't clean enough for a possum.

When the treat was gone, Aloysius leaned his right hip against her knee to wash up, bracing his hands on the floor as she gazed at him adoringly, her hand light against his haunch, whispering that she loved him.

He loved her too, and when he was thoroughly clean, he stretched his pointy white snout up to her face, and clicked as he ran his nose back and forth across her lips.

Chapter 4

Lynda

Ah, the scent of the smaller female opossum drove Aloysius wild. He snuffled and snorted, pressing his pink nose into the distinctive scent on his human's pajama top, clicking loudly and excitedly. His strong hands were fisted in the fabric, and even though his coordination was thrown off by being held in his human's arms, his focus was fixated on that delirious scent, overwhelming him with desire.

Even though the upright position made him dizzy and unbalanced, he had absolutely no fear of falling. The way his human clutched him to her with both arms, he couldn't have pried himself loose if he wanted to, much less fall accidentally. So he followed his nose, searching out every spot in the soft flannel that delicious little Lynda had touched when she had been held in the human's arms earlier.

All too soon, Mom crouched to the floor and slowly, carefully, set Aloysius down on the floor, only releasing him when she was sure he was comfortably standing on his own. Nose high, the six-pound possum followed Lynda's faint trail.

Aloysius inhaled with delight. She had been here, behind the wheel! Blissfully, Aloysius lick-rubbed the solid metal stand of the thing. Finally coming up for air, he clicked loudly, attracting his human's attention. She offered him a dried cherry.

Really? Did he *look* like he was hungry? Aloysius took the treat more to be polite than because he really wanted it, then hitched his way to Lynda's door, raising one hand to test the clear barricade stretching across the doorframe.

His presence brought Lynda over to investigate. Not that she wanted anything to do with him, he was resigned to that; but in hopes that attention meant snacks.

Sure enough, their human reached over the Plexiglas and lifted Lynda up and out, holding her close as she walked to the kitchen to find some sort of goodie.

Settling Lynda on the sofa with a small pile of almonds (where Aloysius couldn't disturb her as she ate), their caretaker set a handful of the delicious nuts in front of Aloysius' nose on the blanket, temporarily distracting him from the wonderful scent of the tiny lady possum. Mom disappeared for a few moments give Ziva! her portion of almonds. (Aloysius never got to interact with Ziva!, but he loved the scent of her on Mom's clothes.)

When Lynda finished her almonds and had spit out the last crescent-shaped pellet of masticated fiber, she stepped from the sofa onto the coffee table. Aloysius abandoned the last of his treat to watch hopefully. Would she come down onto the floor?

Yes! Finding nothing more edible or interesting than an emery board, Lynda slid down the side of the coffee table and set out to search the house. Rapt, Aloysius followed her as best he could, but she was fast, and agile, and only stopped for a few moments here and there, until finally she paused to clean up the scattered kitten chow beneath the starling's cage.

Diplomatically Aloysius approached her from behind, sniffing her tail and hip, then turned his head entirely upside-down to sniff her bottom. Oh, how enchanting! He clicked his adoration, and shoved his nose beneath her hard enough to shift her feet slightly.

Unable to ignore him at this point, Lynda glanced over her shoulder at his wistful self, then moved with surprising swiftness toward her room. At some point their human had slid the barricade away, and Lynda paced through the doorway as if escaping to a different realm.

Aloysius made to follow her, but suddenly Mom was there, and the impervious clear barrier slid between him and beloved little Lynda. He stopped, and clicked in yearning.

The woman gently lifted him up and held him. "I love you, even if she doesn't." She buried her face in his fur, and breathed warm against his fur. "Here, finish your almonds." She set him down with infinite tenderness in front of the almonds he'd forgotten about.

Being a practical possum, Aloysius was soon crunching contentedly, as his human rained gentle kisses on his head and back.

Chapter 5

The New Table

Aloysius clicked, and followed his human around. She was about to leave again; he could tell because she had gotten dressed. The days she spent home with him and the rest of her fur-family, she woke up at about the same time to take the dog out, but then lounged around in her pajamas.

Now she crouched over the small opossum on the floor, tucking his bottom against her knees and leaning her forearms on the floor, on either side of him. He seized one giant hand and lick-rubbed beseechingly.

"Oh, sweetie. I've got to go," she informed him, but made no move to get up, not while he was holding her finger in his tight little fist, and dragging his head backwards over her knuckles.

"Really. I have to be there by quarter to ten."

For such a cute marsupial, Aloysius could be ruthless. He knew as soon as he let go, she'd leave – but he couldn't hang on forever. For one thing, he was thirsty. He gradually relaxed his grip on her finger (leaving little indents) and went over to the water bowl.

She kissed his head, told him she loved him, and stood, then put shoes on, the final step before she abandoned them for the day.

With his hand still on the rim of the water bowl, Aloysius looked up at her and clicked one more time.

She kissed the dog, and went out the door. Resigned, Aloysius scaled the mountain of down comforter in the front of his crate, and settled down inside on the afghan she had knitted for him, to sleep until she came home.

Hours later, Aloysius woke to the sound of the bell on Ziva!'s wheel. He groomed himself awake, then looked, sniffed and listened.

Mom was home! She sat, as she often did, in front of the flat black thing. Happily he climbed up over the blanket and made his way over to her, confident from experience that she would stop whatever she was doing to shower affection upon him.

Wait, what was this, in his path? His human was sitting in her usual spot, but her computer wasn't on the coffee table, but a much shorter table. Aloysius investigated one of its truncated legs. Made of bare wood, it exuded a kaleidoscope of fascinating scents. He slobbered on it and rubbed against it. Oh, that felt good, although the thing moved under his enthusiasm.

Mom steadied it, and held it while he continued. "What do you think, my love? It was at Marie's. You remember Marie?"

Aloysius continued to lick-rub and even bite the table leg in an ecstasy of sensory overload, his eyes defocussing and glazing over, but a small part of his brain heard her. Of course he remembered Marie – Mom used to carry him around in a tote bag, and at Marie's she would give him snacks and smooches.

When he outgrew sleeping in the tote bag, she didn't take him with her anymore. It wasn't comfortable for him to sit on her lap for more than a few minutes, and she wouldn't let him run loose in Marie's house. But he remembered the smell of goats, and treats such as tea, and exotic goat milk cream cheese.

At that thought, his tummy rumbled. Aloysius left off lick-rubbing the table leg and with more determination than grace, climb-hopped up onto Mom's lap. It was dinnertime, and Aloysius had learned not to be too subtle with his human. He sniffed her lips, hoping it was Cheese Night.

As he'd taught her, his human scooped him up and carried him out to the kitchen, where she got a slice of delicious Swiss cheese from the fridge, and fed it to him bite by bite, between kisses.

Chapter 6

The Acupuncture Vet

When his human closed Aloysius in the travel crate he used as his sleeping den, the opossum knew he was being taken somewhere. The last six times his human had thus deprived him of his day's sleep by taking him for a ride in the car, they had gone to see the gentle woman with the soothing touch, whom his human referred to as "Dr. K."

Aloysius liked Dr. K. Whenever he went there (and it seemed less and less frequently), he was given treats and attention, and he had not failed to notice that his right leg seemed stronger and more limber than usual after she made him both tingly and relaxed at the same time with her tiny needles. Confident that this is where they were headed, Aloysius curled up on his afghan and slept to the motion of the car.

He was not disappointed. Mom carried his crate into the vet's office just as a clock like the one at home chimed the hour with ten musical gongs.

Unlike most vet's offices, Dr. K's treatment room was a cozy place with rugs, regular furniture and bookshelves; instead of the smell of antiseptics, Aloysius enjoyed fresh air with a note of lavender; the lighting came from tall windows and incandescent bulbs, not harsh fluorescents; and most of all, there were no other animals present (although he could discern the scent of dozens of different creatures, mostly cats and dogs.) The only sounds were restful music and the vet's cheerful voice.

Aloysius stepped out of his den as soon as Mom opened the door, yawned hugely, then clicked loudly in anticipation of treats, the vet's magic, and another chance to explore this nifty place.

The surface he stepped onto was a nubbly rubber, soft enough to be comfortable, yet sturdy enough for him to grip tightly when his balance deserted him. Happily he accepted piece after piece of cheese from his human, the pleasure of the yummy food intensified by Dr. K's ministrations.

Deftly and thoroughly she ran her hands over his tense little body, and in the wake of her touch came a warmth and relaxation deep inside him. Wide awake now, Aloysius butted his head against his human's hand, his signal to her that he wished to be lifted to the floor.

Ah, training pays off. Immediately she picked him up (trying not to dislodge the many needles) and set him on the carpet with infinite gentleness, a kiss, and a dried cherry.

The little possum sat still while he chewed, concentrating on the pleasure of the treat, then swallowed, gave his hovering human a quick lick-rub of thanks, and set about exploring as the two humans talked quietly, mostly about him.

First stop was the wooden base of the coat tree. Scrutinizing its kaleidoscope of scents, Aloysius applied a layer of saliva to the ornate curve of one leg, and with great enjoyment dragged his head backwards over it, from his silky black ear to his pointy pink nose. He repeated this several times, twisting until he was nearly standing on his head in an attempt to get to just the right spot; then he walked beneath the table and crossed to the wall by the vet's desk, where the wooden floor was edged in a parquet pattern.

The old wooden pieces were skilfully wrought, but some had shifted ever so slightly with age in a way that was delightful to lick-rub. Aloysius went delirious with joy, lick-rubbing until both sides of his jaw were slicked wet to his skin. Mom was there to steady him whenever his coordination failed, as he knew she would be.

Finally Dr. K announced that he was done, and Mom awkwardly slid a hand beneath his tummy and lifted him back up to the table.

Dr. K gave him a head-to-toe massage, plucking out the needles he hadn't shed in his perambulations. She counted them, then assured him that he was a very good patient.

Aloysius shook his fur to neaten it, licked one hand and ran it over his face, then climbed back into the carrier Mom placed in front of him. With another giant yawn, he worked himself under the knitted afghan, and prepared for the long ride home, feeling both rejuvenated and drowsy.

Chapter 7

The (Not So) Great Outdoors

Every evening long after dark, the woman called the large fuzzy dog to the front door and let him go outside. Curious, the opossum often followed, far more interested in the actual door itself than in following the dog. He had had his fill of the outdoors before he was the size of a hamster, and now was glad to be a house opossum.

Inside there were snacks, soft sleeping-spots, and most of all, his surrogate mom. Unlike a real opossum mother, his human had never insisted he manage on his own, and still provided him with food and even groomed him affectionately.

Outside was cold and scary. He knew firsthand that many things wanted to kill him, from owls and foxes to tiny ticks, which might seem insignificant in size, but in large numbers their toll on their unwilling host's blood could be deadly, as he had nearly demonstrated. Occasionally Mom would hold the screen door open, letting Aloysius sniff the breeze. Generally it only took one or two inhales before he spun himself around on his twisted back right leg in a panic and scooted backwards to hide behind the door.

He did like to lick-rub the edge of the inner door as long as the screen door remained shut, and often the big dog had to step carefully around him to get back inside. (Long ago Aloysius had noticed that the retriever would go to great lengths to avoid him, and the opossum was not above occasionally using Arthur's deference to entertain himself at the dog's expense.)

His human seemed satisfied that he wanted nothing to do with going outside, although Aloysius noted that she was very careful to never put this to the ultimate test. Sometimes she carried him outside in her arms, always clutching him tightly, and never, ever allowing a single finger or toe of his to touch dirt. Many times she would just stand there in the dark with him, wrapping him inside her coat with her if it was chilly, as she looked up at the night sky and remarked on the moon or stars, or some event like the meteor shower she had dragged him out to "enjoy" last fall.

Tonight seemed to be another of those nights. When Mom scooped him up and called him her "astronomy opossum," Aloysius essayed to climb right up onto her shoulder in a bid to get her to immediately set him back down on the floor. Instead, she merely peeled him off and rearranged him in her arms once more, and stepped out into the night.

The little opossum could only cling tightly to her, as she walked out from under the trees and looked up at a full moon so bright it cast clearly-defined shadows of the branches on the ground. He knew she would never abandon him in the terrifying wild ... at least he hoped she wouldn't.

Aloysius fidgeted and attempted to burrow inside her pajamas, even though it was warm outside. Next he tried clicking in her ear, then licking her neck, gripping a fistful of her hair so tightly that he felt some of it come loose in his hand. After a few minutes, Mom relented and took him back inside.

Overwhelmed with relief to be back safe and sound, Aloysius caught her hand in both of his, and lick-rubbed her so ecstatically that in his enthusiasm he bit down harder than usual on the fleshy part of her hand by her thumb. Without so much as flinching, she mildly commented, "Ow, it's okay, love."

She kissed him tenderly, apologetically. "I know it's not your favorite, my sweet, but sharing it with you makes it magic. When I'm old I'll cherish my memories of these nights, when you looked at the stars with me." She opened the jar of dried cherries, and he immediately forgave her.

Chapter 8

Pizza!

The small opossum woke to the delectable scent of a pizza in the oven. Only rarely did Mom make pizza, but when she did, she always shared. Aloysius followed his nose out of his crate-den and toward the kitchen.

His human chuckled at the sight of him, up and about long before his usual wakeup time. "It still has fifteen minutes to go, love, and then it has to cool down." She knelt on the floor and cuddled with him, as he raised his pointy white muzzle up to catch the wafting aroma.

"You want a grape while you wait?" In disbelief, Aloysius glanced dismissively at the offering. No, he wanted pizza. With pepperoni. A grape was not an acceptable substitute.

"Ziva! didn't turn down a grape," Mom informed him. Poor Ziva! must truly be starving, Aloysius thought to himself. In an effort to ingratiate himself, he accepted the grape -- only to discover that it was cold. He spit it out, unchewed, onto the rug in front of the sink and turned his back to it. Before the woman could retrieve it, the big dog came along and vacuumed it up, despite (or perhaps because of) the fact that he wasn't supposed to have grapes.

"Well, there's no 'three second rule' in this house," Mom commented wryly.

The big dog and Aloysius had a complicated relationship. Apparently the dog had met an opossum who wasn't as pacifistic as Aloysius, because he would scramble out of the way with far more haste than grace if Aloysius put his face anywhere near the fuzzy gold pup; but when he backed up against the dog, Arthur just ignored him, and allowed the unsteady opossum to brace his butt against him. Clearly, he had encountered sharp marsupial teeth at some point, and learned to avoid them.

Unable to resist, occasionally Aloysius would deliberately approach the dog while he was asleep or inattentive, just for the pleasure of making an eighty-pound dog suddenly leap up and retreat from an eight-pound opossum. It was all the more fun because Aloysius had not the slightest intention of biting.

He had discovered he could also chase the dog from his own dinner bowl. Not that Aloysius craved drool-covered dog kibble, he simply enjoyed watching the big dog back away from his own food. He didn't often get the chance, however, and suspected that Mom deliberately fed the dog when Aloysius wasn't awake yet.

Just then, Mom opened the oven and pulled out the pizza. The droolworthy scent of sauce and cheese suddenly flooded the room, and Aloysius walked over to put one hand on his human's fuzzy-footie-covered foot. Awkwardly she stretched sideways to get a knife out of the drawer without moving that foot.

"It's still hot, love," she said, as he climbed right up onto both of her feet, gripping the fabric of her pajamas in his hand. He heard the distinctive sound of crispy pizza crust being cut and placed into the small unbreakable dishes she used only for opossums.

Sitting patiently at a respectful distance, the dog started to salivate in anticipation. An impressive puddle had collected at his feet by the time Mom declared the pizza safe to eat. She set a bowl with only four small pieces of pizza in front of Aloysius, then stepped over him as he chewed with singleminded concentration, delighting in the spicy sauce, mozzarella, and crust.

Vaguely Aloysius heard a cup of kibble being dumped into the dog's metal bowl, and knew she was feeding the dog while he was distracted, but he didn't care. She had indeed included almost an entire slice of pepperoni in his bowl, and he focused every atom of his being on the rare treat, taking his time to enjoy it thoroughly, as possums are wont to do.

With his raspy tongue, he licked the bowl so clean it was dry, then backed up against Mom's foot to wash his face and clean his teeth. Maybe he could coax another tidbit of pizza later in the small hours of the night, when Mom was sleepy and inclined to indulge the little possum.

He clicked and rubbed his head against her ankle, then made his way to the dog's water bowl, just as the dog started to drink. Startled, the dog skittered backwards in mid-lap, trailing water. Aloysius took possession of the bowl with one hand and a regal air, and drank.

Chapter 9

Possum Magic

Mom was ignoring him for the laptop again. She stared at the screen and made tapping sounds with her fingers while Aloysius tried to get her attention. The little table she sat crosslegged in front of was made of unfinished wood – delightful for lick-rubbing – so he threw his whole self into it, his eyes glazing over in ecstasy as he drew his face backwards against one short leg of the thing, plastering the fur on his jawline flat with saliva, and giving himself a really impressive pseudo-mohawk on top.

She couldn't really ignore him when the whole table rocked beneath his efforts, but she petted him absently, instead of dropping what she was doing to give him the intense full-focused attention he was accustomed to and craved.

So Aloysius moved on to lick-rubbing his human's shins, wetting down her pajamas. Surely she must notice that! He stood back and clicked at her.

"Wow, that's a lot of possum spit," she commented, stroking him nose to tail several times before she continued typing.

He lick-rubbed her foot in its fuzzy sock. She chuckled, and offered him some dried fruit, but quickly returned to her keyboard.

He refused the treat. What made this nonliving plastic thing more important than him?

The small opossum had had enough. He wanted real petting, not distracted half-measures and bribes of food. Resolutely he climbed right up into her lap, and sniffed at the front of her pajama top. Yes, he could tell she had held both female opossums in the last hour or so, but that wasn't what he was after.

Mom quit typing, and lightly encircled his uncoordinated body with her hands. Encouraged, Aloysius clicked, and rubbed his pink nose along her lips, tasting the chocolate she had been eating. (Sometimes she shared chocolate.)

She scooted out away from the table, holding him upright against her chest with his bottom braced on her lap. Pulling off her glasses and dropping them to the blanket beside her, she brought her knees up and gently, carefully leaned the little possum backwards against her thighs, and buried her nose in the yellow-tinged fur of his chest, steadying him with her hands on his forearms.

She inhaled slowly and deeply of the virile scent, holding her breath for a long moment before finally releasing it in a soft hum of pleasure. "You are magic, my little love," she informed him, drawing another deep drag of the sharp, musky aroma. "Mmmmm."

Satisfied that he at last had her undivided attention, Aloysius gripped Mom's ear in one fist, and gave the side of her head a quick rub.

"Ow?" she said, but made no move to pry his fingers off. Instead she leaned down further and exhaled warm breath into the ultra-soft fur of his tummy. "I love you, Aloysius."

When he let go of her ear, she pulled back enough to gaze into his face. "I'm not really ignoring you," she told him. "In fact, I'm writing about you, so I can remember every detail, for always."

The small opossum vigorously licked the hand holding his left arm, and clicked at her. When she offered him the dried cherry again, this time he took it, rearranged it in his mouth with his hand, then chewed with his eyes squinched shut in sheer pleasure.

Chapter 10

Into the Fridge

Aloysius did not like the feeling of having a wet bottom. His twisted spine made his back left leg slide beneath him, so unless he peed directly over the shower drain, his foot slid and he ended up getting soaked. If he had to, he could clean himself, but Mom would cheerfully do it for him, faster and with affection and snacks.

The small possum headed for his human where she slept on the floor with a sleeping retriever draped over her legs. Aloysius skirted the dog without baiting him. Awake, the dog was harmless, and the possum enjoyed making him move out of his way; but if startled from sleep, the eighty-pound retriever was clumsy and prone to overreacting. While he might not mean to hit the little possum, Aloysius wasn't fast or agile enough to evade a flailing foot, and it hurt to be kicked, however unintentional it might be.

Skirting around the dog, Aloysius made his way to his human's head. She braided her hair before she went to sleep, and the texture of her hair pulled flat against her head was perfect for lick-rubbing. Ahh. Aloysius licked and rubbed his head on hers, climbing half on top of her face to get the right angle, using her nose as a step.

It wasn't always easy to wake his human, but she soon had her hands around his middle to steady him even if she wasn't fully awake. The little possum clicked at her as she opened her eyes.

"What do you need, my little love? You want a snack?" She felt his bottom out of habit, and immediately came to full alertness, and pulled a soft kleenex from the box on the table. "Hang on, let's get you some soap and water," she said, blotting most of the wet off him. Carrying him out to the kitchen, she ran warm water over a paper towel, added a bit of hand soap, and gently wiped his bottom.

Aloysius stood patiently while she cleaned him up and then used a couple fresh kleenex to dry him off. This always made him feel like a tiny joey, and he liked being the focus of her love and solicitude. Once clean, however, he had another idea.

Clicking at her, he walked to the refrigerator and sat in front of it, shifting his hands back and forth. The Swiss cheese was kept in there, a special treat for midnight snacking.

"You want some leftover eggs?" Mom asked, shifting him to one side so she could open the door.

Ah, the fridge was open! Aloysius eagerly climbed up onto the lower ledge, hoping to show her where the cheese was.

Briefly he glanced at the eggs, then raised his pointy nose toward the cheese drawer and sniffed hopefully.

"You want some Swiss cheese?" she asked. Aloysius clicked his approval, and she unwrapped one delicious slice. "Can you move a little, so I can shut the door?" she asked, leading him with a bite-size piece. He took a few steps and accepted the treat, chewing with satisfaction as she carefully shut the fridge door behind him.

He knew she set aside part of the slice for the other possums, and even fed a substantial hunk to the dog, but Aloysius concentrated on the good things he got. Piece after piece he ate all she gave him, then washed up as she went to share the treat with the two girls.

Chapter 11

Egg Night with Au Gratin Potatoes

Most wild opossums eat everything raw, unless they have the great good fortune to happen across something in a garbage bin; while that was fine for his wild brethren, one of the many things little Aloysius appreciated about his human was that she sure knew how to cook.

Take tonight's dinner, for example. It appeared to be simple scrambled eggs, which of course are delicious, but oh, it was so much more. Mom melted a tablespoon of real butter in the pan before cracking in the eggs – and what eggs! These were none of those stale storebought eggs from factory farms, with pastel yolks and no flavor. Oh, no. These were tiny Arucana eggs (Mom had shown them to him) from chickens that roamed freely about the goat farm run by Mom's dear friend, Marie. The yolks were a deep orange and full of deliciousness.

Mom also added calcium with vitamin D to the eggs before they were cooked. She thought she was being sneaky, but it takes a lot to outsmart a possum. It wasn't that Aloysius and the girls were unaware of the supplements, it was just that they didn't mind the slightly chalky texture.

And, the crowning touch: once the eggs were thoroughly cooked, Mom sprinkled on a luscious blend of shredded cheese to melt and mingle most yummily. Everyone loved Egg Night.

Tonight, in addition to the scrumptious eggs, his human had used the oven (generally a harbinger of good things) making the whole house smell of potato and cheese. Aloysius had even dreamed of this, right before waking up, inspired by the rich heavenly scent.

Another thing the undersized opossum loved about his human was that she would cheerfully share anything she was eating. Tonight he had enjoyed a small taste of the cheese-and-potato recipe served with his eggs, but when he noticed that Mom was eating some herself from her own bowl, he meandered over.

"Aloysius? Are you under the table?" she asked, leaning sideways to peer at him. He clicked in greeting, and also because he could tell that she had been holding each of the girls. He waited with confident expectation. Simply presenting himself when she had food was usually all the prompt that was needed.

She was so well-trained! It didn't take long for her to spear a small piece with her fork and offer it to Aloysius. Long accustomed to eating off utensils, the small possum took the food and fork together into his wide mouth, delicately biting down just to the metal, and scraping the treat off with his teeth.

Several times she refilled the fork, then she set the empty bowl in front of him. Gripping the edge with one dextrous hand, Aloysius licked the bowl completely clean, then climbed up into her lap to wash his face and hands.

Chapter 12

The Ring Perch and the Hawk

One of the little possum's favorite items to lick-rub was the metal ring perch with its six legs radiating out from the center. It smelled of many different birds, some of the scents very old, some new, all of them intriguing to Aloysius in his nightly serial lick-rub-athon. The painted metal was cool to his tongue as he licked one of the supports, laying down a layer of saliva; then he dragged his face backwards across the top of the thing, over and over, enjoying the sound of the leash ring clinking against the center post. He stopped in consternation when the leg suddenly came loose from the base, and rolled uselessly when he tried to rub his head on it.

Mom could fix it. He went to get her, where she was sitting on a blanket on the floor with the dog and a book. Climbing right up onto her leg, he put a hand on her novel and clicked at her, loudly. In answer she set down the paperback, and scooped him completely into her lap. Aloysius clicked and rubbed his face on her hand. Would she get the hint?

Nope, she either had no idea what he wanted, or was pretending to not know, as an excuse to hold him. He swayed back and forth, his balance deserting him – then he smelled that luscious scent of

28

female opossum. Still dizzy but now focused with determination, he grabbed Mom's flannel top in one strong hand, and sniffed insistently at the fabric. Here, and *here*! He found several spots with Lynda's delicate scent, so rich, so intoxicating, so *female*.

His human knew he wanted to scrutinize those scents, but also understood his coordination difficulties; she scooched around so she could slowly lay flat on her back, with the diminutive possum standing on her chest instead of being held upright to sniff those interesting smells. Aloysius appreciated her thoughtfulness, and clicked his thanks.

After a few minutes of intense sniffing, he stepped down from her shoulder to the floor. The metal lick-rub item still needed to be fixed. Clicking to get his human to follow him, he headed back to the perch.

"You unscrewed it again?" she asked, bending to put it back together. "There you go," she said, as Aloysius checked it out, testing the leg with a couple of vigorous rubs. Ah, all better. He resumed his interrupted lick-rub.

A few days later, when Aloysius walked past the perch to get to the water bowl, he stopped in surprise. There was a new hawk scent on the thing, very fresh, only hours old. The same feather-smell he sometimes caught on Mom's hands or face in the morning, the distinct touch of the Cooper's Hawk that lived outside.

But today she had been inside, right here – standing on the little possum's second-favorite lick-rub item (Mom being his first) as if she owned it. He reached a hand up to steady himself on the lower part of the round armature, inhaling the warm birdsmell on the rope wrapping the top half. There it was, bold as brass. He snorted.

"Yes, I brought Alice in the house earlier, and she sat on it for awhile," Mom informed him, offering him half a grape. "It is, technically, a hawk perch." Mom always cut his grapes in half.

Recognizing the grape as a ploy to distract him, he took it anyway, chewing with pleasure. He didn't really mind the bird sitting on the perch, it was just different, and interesting, but he cheerfully allowed Mom to change the subject with this yummy treat. After extracting all the flavor from the juicy morsel, he spit out the bitter skin, and begged for more with zero shame.

Chapter 13

Cheese Night and Lickrubs

It was dark outside, but Mom had yet to make dinner. She sat staring at the computer screen as she had been for hours now, reading – sometimes crying, sometimes laughing, sometimes writing something down in the notebook she kept on the coffee table. Somebody had to do something, and the little opossum figured it was apparently up to him, since the big dog would never presume to interrupt their human for something as insignificant as dinner as long as he could lay up against her and be petted occasionally.

Aloysius didn't consider meals insignificant, so he roused himself and slowly climbed out over the down comforter in the doorway of his crate-den. Clicking softly, he walked beneath the short table to lickrub her shin briefly, then climbed up into her crosslegged lap.

"Aloysius!" she greeted him, scooting backwards to give him room, her computer novel instantly set aside. He clicked louder, and touched her lips with his wet pink nose.

"Mmm, I love when you kiss me," she murmured into his left ear, the one with the piece missing. She scooped him up and headed for the kitchen.

Setting him down on the carpet in front of the sink, she rummaged around in the refrigerator. "How about Cheese Night?" she asked, offering a small cube of Meunster cheese for his approval.

Aloysius loved Meunster cheese. He accepted it and chewed with his eyes half closed to better concentrate on the delicious taste.

She laughed gently and ruffled his fur. "I'll take that as a 'yes,' then," she smiled at him. He heard bowls rattling and plastic crinkling, and then a bowl of cheese cubes appeared before his nose. He sniffed them, but made no move to take one; instead, the small opossum waited expectantly to be served by hand.

"You really won't eat out of the bowl," she said, hunkering down to fold herself around him, and he could hear the pleasure in her voice that he preferred to be handfed. She handed him each piece, one at a time, breathing into his fur and kissing him as he chewed unhurriedly. When the bowl was empty and no more cheese was forthcoming, Aloysius lick-rubbed her hand, pinning her arm to the floor with one hand on her wrist.

He approached this task with great seriousness and vigor, sometimes getting rather carried away and mouthing or biting her, but she never reproached him, and never, *ever* removed her hand before he was done. He rarely drew blood, and she didn't even seem to mind when he did.

Eventually he let go, and she straightened to finish building dinners. Aloysius washed up, then lickrubbed the top of her foot several times.

She stood with one foot on either side of him, bracketing him with her protection. Aloysius loved the feeling of being cherished, and just sat between her feet with his right hand on her right instep, silent and still and thoughtful, clicking quietly to himself periodically.

Chapter 14

Henge Possum

Aloysius followed the enticing scent of ham out of his sleeping-spot. He should have known better.

As he chewed, he looked around, and gradually realized with some concern that his human was wearing a coat over her pajamas. Why did she want him out of his bed when she was going outside? Usually she sought the reassurance of knowing that he was comfortably asleep before she departed.

Did it have something to do with her newest yard project? She and the gentle oaf of a dog had spent over an hour outside after she came home from work, but they'd been moving around in the woods behind the house instead of going for a walk. and when they had finally come back inside, they'd smelled of dead leaves, stones, and damp black leaf mulch. (The dog had brought actual leaves inside, stuck to his fuzzy coat.)

"Aloysius, wait till you see! I put up the stones," she informed him. She wanted him to see something – outside? Well, that couldn't be good, the little possum thought with some trepidation. Far too late, he tried to make it to the comfort and safety of his crate-den.

His human scooped him up, grabbed his afghan from his bed, and kissed the top of his head. "Just one picture, love. Just one. Then I'll bring you right back inside," she promised.

Why do you have to take me out at all? The little possum wondered, struggling to regain his balance as she carried him out the front door into the deepening dark of evening.

"I just want to be able to think of you out there, and have a picture to remind me," she explained, as if she heard his thoughts. Maybe she did. She walked through the litter of last year's leaves, the sound loud in the quiet.

It was pleasantly cool outside, with a light breeze off the lake and some scattered birdsong; but Aloysius just wanted to go back home.

After a few more paces, she called the dog over and bid him stay; then she arranged the blue afghan near a medium-size rock, and, to Aloysius' disbelief and horror, set him down. Outside. On the ground (well, almost.) Then she backed away! She was leaving him there!

In a panic he scrambled toward her, but she easily stopped him and rearranged him on the blanket. "Just one picture, love. Just one," she repeated. "Please?" Even as she pleaded, he could hear the whine of the camera flash charging, and then sure enough, the bright light he knew so well temporarily blinded him.

Immediately Mom gathered him up in her arms, hugging him tightly to her, covering his face with kisses as she hurried back to the house. In moments she was setting him down on the rug by the kitchen sink, and produced a bite of his favorite sliced Swiss cheese. "Thank you, sweetie, thank you," she murmured into his silken silver fur.

Aloysius recognized an edible apology when one was handed to him, and accepted it graciously. After a few more bites, she went back outside alone with her camera, returning in a few minutes with a grin. "I love our little henge, sweetie," she said, curling up over Aloysius and smooching him some more.

"The setting sun determined the West stone, then I lined up the East one with that first one and the stump in the center, using a string to keep them the same distance from the center. North and South were at right angles to the first two, then I kind of guessed at the intermediary four. And now you've personally been there and imbued it with your *seiðr*, your magic. Mmmm, you are so sweet to me," she nuzzled his nose and he clicked. "I love you, Aloysius."

The small opossum had forgiven her with the first bite of cheese; now he reached up to catch the sleeve of her pajama top in one dextrous little hand, and lick-rubbed her shoulder over and over, only letting go when the flannel was soaked through and sticking to her skin, and his face was sopping wet.

She kissed him anyway, and he clicked back at her.

Chapter 15

The Interloper

The sounds of morning activity brought the small opossum up out of sleep. He lay between drowsing and waking, debating whether to get up, when he felt Mom's hand on his side. He licked her knuckles, then settled more comfortably into the hand-knitted afghan and down comforter, and gave a deep contented sigh.

Eyes closed, he followed his human's movements by sound. She fed the dog, and filled his water bowl. She washed her hair and got dressed.

Then, close to his den, he heard the barricade to Ziva!'s doorway slide open, and then Mom was talking quietly to Ziva!, and Aloysius heard crunching. Sounds of the glider cage being cleaned followed ... Aloysius suddenly woke to full alertness. He had not heard the barricade being closed.

He had never been in Ziva!'s room.

Quietly he crept from his bed (although he would have stoutly denied any attempt to be stealthy) and stepped around the clear plastic that normally blocked him from entering, but which now stood ajar. His whole marsupial being alight with keen curiosity, Aloysius strode into the hitherto-forbidden room, taking his time to sniff and investigate a snake cage, a closet – was that a cage of *roaches* on the floor in there? – a water bowl, and a fleecy blanket on the floor with a toy opossum on it.

Mom sat facing the wheel in the corner, taping paper towels to the inner surface and folding the edges over. Aloysius clicked and walked up to her.

"Aloysius!" she said, in pleased surprise, glancing at the wooden hut that Ziva! slept in.

He put a hand on her leg, and peered at the paper towels on the wheel. Why was she doing that? His wheel didn't have paper towels on it.

"The girls sometimes pee on their wheels," Mom explained, as she put a few pieces of tape on the outside surface, tacking down the folded corners.

Then the delicate pointy nose of Ziva! herself showed in the overstuffed doorway of the hut, and Mom stood up, hovering. As soon as Ziva! had fully emerged, Mom scooped her up in her arms, smooched her soundly, and set her on the bed. A few pieces of dog kibble kept her there, while Aloysius watched from the floor, clicked, and yearned to sniff her exquisite self.

Finishing her treat, Ziva! walked over to the edge of the bed to look down on him with frank annoyance. Undeterred, Aloysius came over to the corner and stretched his nose upwards, but knew of course that he couldn't climb up. She leaned over, clearly considering him an interloper in her domain.

He just wanted a sniff or two ... but he didn't even get within a foot of her nose before Mom gathered him up and took him out of the room, closing the barricade and latching it securely behind them.

"I'm sorry, love, she wouldn't be nice to you," his human whispered into his pink-tipped ear. "You can help me clean Lynda's room, though." She set him down in front of Lynda's room, and slid open that barricade.

Aloysius had been in Lynda's room many times, but it never lost its appeal. He preceded Mom in and sniffed around, looking for the tiny female whose scent covered everything.

As she had with Ziva!'s wheel, Mom stripped off the old paper towels and taped down new ones. Aloysius supervised, then took a few steps on it after Mom pronounced it done. It was much smaller than his and the paper towels felt odd beneath his hands and feet, but he clicked his approval.

He then lick-rubbed the wooden magazine holder with its intricate design, took a few laps of water from the bowl nearby, and gave a quick lickrub on the cover of the romance novel Lynda had pulled out of the bookshelf during the night.

But he couldn't find Lynda. Perplexed, he went to his human and gazed up in entreaty.

"Lynda's way in the bottom of the sleeping bag, sweetheart," the woman told him, hunching down to wrap her arms around him and kiss him. "She won't come out till tonight."

Disappointed, Aloysius followed Mom out of the room, and headed for his wheel to walk off his frustration.

Chapter 16

Bad Dream

Aloysius growled.

Suddenly, a human was there with soft words and a gentle touch. Aloysius woke up, still disoriented, cornered in a small space, being touched. He showed his teeth — impressive now that he was nearly ten months old — and growled again. Loudly.

The woman slowly withdrew her hand from his crate with a heartbroken, quiet word: "Aloysius?"

The eight-pound opossum got his feet beneath him and blinked, shaking off the last of the nightmare. He couldn't even remember what it had been about now. He took a step toward his human, recognizing her now as Mom, the one who loved him no matter what he did, took care of his every need and want, gave him smooches and good things to eat, and occasionally annoyed him. He loved her.

Now she looked scared, and it was because of him. "Aloysius? Are you all right? Are you okay?" she asked, fear in her voice. She got up and left.

In a few moments she returned with a slice of Swiss cheese. "You want some cheese?" she asked, offering a bite-size piece.

Aloysius stepped forward a pace and accepted the tidbit, chewing happily. She held out another, making him reach for it, and he knew what she was doing: she was drawing him out of his sleeping cave, but he wanted that cheese (also, he had to pee.) He took another step and another bite. Mmm.

Soon only the tip of his tail was still inside his travel crate, and as he expected, Mom picked him up, almost gingerly, pulled off her glasses and gazed into his eyes. "Are you okay, love? I need you to be okay. I need you," she mumbled that last into the fur of his shoulder, and he could feel his fur getting wet.

She stood still with him for a long moment, then asked, "You want to eat dinner on the sofa with Lynda? You love Lynda," she said, setting him tenderly on the couch. She went to the library, where Lynda was already at the barricade, having smelled that tonight they were having broccoli chicken.

Aloysius could see and smell Lynda as Mom carried her out to the kitchen, returning with Lynda and her dinner, which Lynda had already started.

Holding the small female so he could barely reach her tail with his nose, Mom asked, "You're okay, right? You're not going to growl or bite Lynda?"

Aloysius clicked in reply. Of course not. He loved Lynda, and Mom too. The bad dream was forgotten.

Mom placed Lynda down next to him on the sofa, and Aloysius sniffed her deliriously as she chewed giant bites with her mouth open. Mom watched for a few seconds, as if ready to snatch the tiny female from his jaws, but Aloysius merely clicked, and sniffed, and sneezed.

Deciding Lynda was safe, the woman went out to the kitchen again, returning with his familiar black dish.

"Would you eat some broccoli chicken for me, my love?" She set a dish of warm chicken with cheese sauce and broccoli in front of his nose, and watched closely as he pulled the bowl toward him with one hand and took a piece.

Chewing with singleminded enjoyment together, the two opossums ate in comfortable companionship — until Lynda finished first. Without hesitation or remorse, she dove into his half-eaten meal and polished it off with amazing efficiency. Aloysius didn't mind. He frankly abandoned his meal in favor of sniffing her delicious female self.

Gently he licked her ear, and clicked softly, in entreaty. She ignored him, washed up with more haste than hygiene, then escaped his persistent affection by stepping from the sofa onto the coffee table. She had interacted with him often enough to know he could"t follow across the foot-wide chasm between the two.

But Mom was right there, and scooped up her beloved little girl just as Lynda reached for the mug full of candy. Smooching her soundly, the woman returned Lynda to the library, latched the barricade, and handed her several pieces of dried fruit. Then she knelt by the side of the sofa.

"You ate, you acted normal with Lynda, you seem to be okay?" she asked more than stated. Aloysius came over to sniff her pajama top, where Lynda had been. Mom picked up his bowl and went back to the kitchen, returning shortly with half a dish of chicken, about what he'd allowed Lynda to pilfer.

Appreciative as always, the small opossum sat and ate unhurriedly while she fussed over him, but he could tell she was no longer scared and crying. Really, he didn't know what else he could do to reassure her. When he was done, he leaned against her arm to wash up, doing a thorough job of it, even including her hand in his ministrations, hoping to allay her fears.

To his dismay, this made her start crying into his fur again (the fur he had just spent ten minutes grooming!) — but this time she was thanking him for being all right, and they were happy tears.

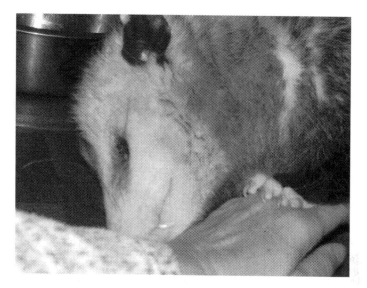

Chapter 17

Meteor Shower

"Where's my favorite astronomy possum?" Mom asked.

Aloysius stilled and watched with wary suspicion as his human shrugged into her coat. It was dark outside, and Mom never called him that particular nickname after dark unless she intended to drag him out into the night to stare up at the starry sky.

Aloysius frankly disliked the outdoors; the smells and sounds, the feel of it, brought back too many terrifying memories. Unfortunately, that didn't stop the woman from dragging him along on these astronomical and astronomically asinine forays — although to be fair, it wasn't very often. She crouched down and slid her hands beneath his chest and bottom, lifting him off his feet to press him tightly to her and wrap her coat around him.

The small opossum clung with all the strength in his fingers, toes and tail as the movement caused a disorienting dizziness to temporarily overwhelm him. Vaguely he was aware she had opened the inner door.

He recalled that the dog had radiated cold when he came back in just now, so it was chilly outside to boot. There was nothing about this whole venture that wasn't unpleasant.

They stepped outside, and the dizziness dissipated as sharp air hit his face. He was grateful that Mom had wrapped him up inside her coat, and burrowed down in as she paced to the middle of the front yard and stopped.

"Wow, look at all the stars," she said. Aloysius ignored both her and and her stupid stars, hoping she'd soon see whatever it was she was looking for this time and they could go back in before his pinned-back ears developed frostbite.

"Tonight's supposed to be the best night for the meteor shower," she informed him, kissing the tense little possum in her arms. Slowly she turned in a full circle, head tilted back toward the sky. "And not a cloud in the sky, although it was raining this afternoon. Wow, what luck —"

Aloysius growled low in this throat at the dim shape that approached from around the corner of the house with alarming speed and stealth. It was a cat, and a large one. All too aware of his smaller-than-normal size, the eight-pound opossum tried to climb onto Mom's shoulder, but she held him firmly in place. After a short struggle, he gave up and growled again.

"Aloysius?" Mom asked, uncertain. "What's wrong?"

Didn't she see the giant cat right at her feet?

"Are you upset about Sly Cat? You know Sly," she said, in a reasonable tone.

Not out here, he didn't. A cat asleep on the sofa in the sun all afternoon was one thing; skulking about in the dark of night was a whole different creature entirely. He growled louder.

"Okay, okay, we'll go back in," his human suddenly, finally figured it out. Hastily she rattled the screen door and pushed open the heavy inside door, then shut it behind them.

Aloysius immediately quieted. This growling thing seemed to be a useful training tool. He had just shortened what could have been a half an hour ordeal to three and a half minutes, although she had yet to set him down.

He sighed. He knew she cherished holding him, but largely refrained from doing so because of his balance issues. Now, however, he was already comfortably settled in her arms, so he allowed her to stand for a long moment, hugging him so tightly that it was a good thing marsupials can tolerate low oxygen levels, because he could barely breathe.

Eventually she relaxed her suffocating embrace, knelt and transferred him gently to the floor, folding herself over him to encircle him in her arms. "I'm sorry, love, I never meant to scare you. I've seen meteors, I know what they look like, we don't have to stand outside and watch."

Reassured that his human could learn from her mistakes, Aloysius put a hand on her wrist and lifted his pointy muzzle up toward her. As he'd taught her, she responded by leaning her head right down to the floor in front of him, so he could lick-rub her hair, which he did with great gusto, tangling her braid and soaking her head with possum spit.

Chapter 18

Monthiversary

Aloysius didn't really understand the concept of "monthiversary," but he certainly understood scrambled eggs with cheese and oh, was that HAM? Only very rarely did he or any of the critters (or even Mom herself) ever get ham. Delicately he accepted a mouthful of the luscious treat from his human's fingers, his inch-long fangs barely touching her skin. It was so delicious that he squinted in pleasure as he chewed, savoring the taste although he was starving. He was eating much later than usual tonight.

Mom was much clingier than usual as well, following him about, constantly touching him, stroking his sides, kissing him. Usually she spent at least part of the night sleeping, but tonight something had happened.

Aloysius still wasn't sure what. When he woke up at his regular time, he had been pleased to find Lynda on the blanket by the coffee table, and sniffed her delectable self as she ate. Ignoring the second bowl of food, he headed for Lynda's room (which Mom grandly referred to as "the library" on the strength of a single overflowing bookshelf.) He'd just begun lick-rubbing Lynda's sleeping bag when he suddenly felt ... odd.

Next thing he knew, it was over an hour later. He still felt odd, disoriented and dizzy, but now he was under the art desk, the house was dark, and Lynda was barricaded back in the library. Mom was stroking his fur and talking low and softly to him, her tone suggesting she had been doing so for some time. There was a distinct taste of tears in her voice, and he himself seemed to be the focus of her distress.

As most wild animals will, the small opossum valiantly ignored the peculiar uneasy sensation, and instead clicked at the woman and licked her hand. In response, she lifted him up with exaggerated tenderness, and held him against her heart, murmuring to him, "I love you, Aloysius. I love you. I love you."

The strange episode had eclipsed his usual discomfort at being picked up, and he relaxed into her embrace, clicking and rubbing his cold, wet nose against her own warm, dry one. She pressed her face to his chest and inhaled deeply of the clean, musky scent of him, holding her breath for several seconds before exhaling. She often behaved as if he were some sort of addictive drug, and truth be told, he liked it.

Only after ascertaining that he was acting normally did she produce the dish of ham and eggs, which Aloysius cheerfully polished off with alacrity. He then toddled over to his personal water dish (verboten to the dog, so it stayed clean and fresh all night long) and stood on unsteady legs to lap up a nice long drink.

"You're okay now, my love?" his human asked, her eyes still wet with tears.

He could feel her fearful uncertainty, and sought to reassure her with a lickrub. Climbing right up onto her lap as she sat crosslegged on the floor, he put a hand on her wrist and gave a quick lick, then dragged his head back and forth across her knuckles, still clicking.

As she sometimes did, she leaned back to lay on the floor, with Aloysius standing on her stomach. He sniffed her bathrobe with interest, noting where Lynda and Ziva! had been held recently, then he stepped off her stomach onto the blanket. He was still hungry, and gazed at her in a silent yet eloquent entreaty for a snack.

"Hang on," Mom said, and went out to the kitchen. The little opossum heard plastic crinkle, then she returned with a bowl of grapes (cut in half, of course), banana, apple, broccoli, a brussels sprout and almonds. Almonds he was willing to eat straight out of the bowl, so he sat and chewed and spit out the fiber, while Mom gently leaned her forehead against his, her hands on his shoulders.

When he couldn't find any more almonds, he leaned against those loving arms and washed up, smoothing the fur on his haunches, and using one back foot to dig delicately into his ear. The full tummy and extensive grooming completed his transition back to normalcy, and Aloysius ran his nose across Mom's lips with a loud click, eliciting a happy "mmm" from her.

"There's a cookie, too," Mom informed him, showing him the crescent-shaped, banana-scented baked treat. She broke it into several manageable bites, and fed them to him one by one. "Happy monthiversary, my love," she said, kissing him reverently on top of his head.

Aloysius clicked at her, then scooted backwards to brace his butt against her hand. Now he had to wash up all over again.

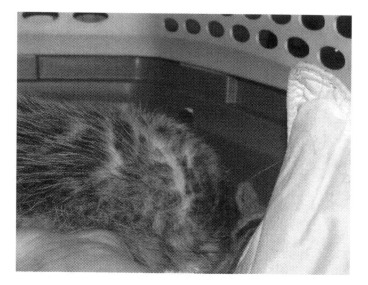

Chapter 19

Sleeping Together

Curled up half-asleep in the dark nook beneath the chair, the small opossum was unsurprised to feel his human's hand gently stroke his side. He captured her hand with his own, licked her fingers and laid his head in her palm, relaxing back into the fleecy blanket with a deep sigh of contentment.

A little over two hours later, he woke, licked her hand again, and climbed out of the cozy sleeping-spot to sniff her face. She didn't wake. He clicked, and ran his nose along her lips. That woke her up. Mom pulled her arm back from beneath the chair to pet him symmetrically, one hand on each side so as not to disrupt his uneasy balance.

"Ow, ow, ow," she groaned as she moved her arm. She often put herself in pretzel positions for the pleasure of petting him while he slept, and paid the price in pain afterwards. She kissed the side of his face. "Mmmm."

Aloysius just sat there and clicked.

"You want your dinner?" she asked, sleepily. "It's Cheese Night, my love."

Well, yes, he'd figured out all on his own that it was Cheese Night by the bowl of cubed Meunster sitting next to his water bowl a scant two feet away. His human had a gift for stating the obvious, but Aloysius generously chalked it up to sleep deprivation. If she slept during the day like a normal creature, she wouldn't have this problem.

She picked up a piece of cheese from the bowl and offered it to him with a nonverbal question. "Hmmm?"

Aloysius clicked and rubbed the back of his head against her hand once. Nope.

"Okay, let's see what else we've got," she said, getting to her feet and heading for the kitchen. The big dog tagged along, hoping for handouts. The little possum trailed behind them, with a definite goal in mind.

"How about almonds, you love almonds," Mom said, setting a paper towel in front of him, then pouring a handful of almonds on it.

He looked at them, then at her. This was not what he'd been hoping for.

She crouched down and offered him one from her fingers. "You really don't want an almond?"

He shoved his pointy nose against her arm.

"Okaaaay," his human said, drawing the word out as she gathered up the almonds, stood, and opened the cupboard.

"Ah ha. How about a nanner cookie?" She rattled some plastic and produced the very treat desired, breaking its crescent shape into four bite-size chunks.

Cheerfully Aloysius accepted a piece of the delicious tidbit, turning and backing up a pace to get his feet stabilized beneath him. She crouched over him as he chewed, and fed him the remaining pieces one by one, smooching his head and shoulders as he ate the final bite.

Tummy satisfied, he hiked over to the dog bowl and assessed its potability. She must have cleaned and refilled it recently, for it had a relatively low level of slimy dog spit. Deeming it tolerable, he drank his fill, then headed for his crate.

Barely had he climbed in and burrowed into the soft afghan when he heard Mom spread a blanket next to the crate, and set the alarm clock nearby. (The latter meant that she had to leave in the morning.) Then she lay down with her head on the end of his down comforter sticking out of the crate, flipped half the blanket over herself, and gently reached inside to pet him.

Far from objecting to this intrusion on his personal space, Aloysius loved the attention, the affection. He clicked softly, gave her hand a few drowsy licks, then flopped over onto his side on her arm, ending up with the side of his head cradled in her hand, his favorite pillow.

Chapter 20

Another New Table

Through the haze of midday sleep, the little possum was vaguely aware of strangers in the house, something heavy being brought in and assembled with a whining power tool, then, blissfully, quiet after they left. He heard/smelled Mom going over the new item with hot soapy water, but it seemed too much trouble to get up and see what it was. He'd check it out later. He turned over and went back to sleep.

That evening, waking to the delightful smell of scrambled eggs, Aloysius clambered out of his doorless crate with some difficulty over the down comforter he'd pulled in after himself. Once on the floor, he clicked to himself in satisfaction, and set out for the dog's water bowl. Leaning hard on the edge of the thing, he lowered his nose to drink. Without warning, the whole thing tipped beneath his hand, and he felt the shock of cold water running over his feet and hands.

Within moments, Mom was there, scooping him up. "Are you okay, love?" She set him down on the soft possum towel and tenderly dried him off. Then she picked him up again and took him over to his personal water dish by her pillow, kissed him for a long moment, then set him down. An uninitiated observer might have thought she was being kind, but the little possum knew it was really just an excuse to hold him. Still, he was thirsty, and the water was clean and fresh. He lapped eagerly.

Meanwhile, the woman picked up the ring perch and dog bowls, dried the floor with the dog towel, and set everything aside so the floor could dry, tossing the dripping floral placemat into the washing machine. Finishing his drink, Aloysius toddled over to supervise.

Ah, the ring perch! He headed for it, only to halt in surprise at the table towering over him in the corner that had always been empty. Its center post and feet were made of metal, like the ring perch, only with a texture unlike anything he had ever encountered. Not rough, but not smooth, it looked just right for lick-rubbing, and he proceeded to test this theory.

Soon his eyes had glazed over and his cheek-fur was plastered to his skin with saliva. He blinked and gradually came to, hearing Mom's voice through his self-induced delirium, finally making out words.

"You're hitting your magnificent fangs on the floor, love," she worried, anxiously feeling his upper canines. Her touch was gentle but annoying, squeezing the sides of his nose like that. Aloysius lick-rubbed her hand, clicking loudly. He didn't mind if his teeth touched the floor once in awhile. Contrary to what Mom seemed to think, he wasn't made of glass; he was the product of seventy million years of evolutionary success, sabertooth fangs and all.

Still, to placate her, he moved away from the wonderful metal table legs, investigating the wooden chair legs next. Ah, these were also excellent for lick-rubbing! He went at it with alacrity and vigor, discovering that while the table had not moved at all, he could shove the chair several inches with each delightful drag of his head.

Mom sat on her heels and watched, taking pictures. Early in life he had grown inured to the random flashes of bright light that usually accompanied anything new or interesting.

After chasing the chair for a good couple of feet, Aloysius turned his back on the new table, and climbed up into Mom's lap to thank her for the nifty new toy. She welcomed him by wrapping her arms around him and kissing the top of his head, as he lick-rubbed her hands. Again.

Chapter 21

Late!

Mom was usually home by the time Aloysius woke up, even if she stopped at the store; but now it was already seven o'clock, and still no Mom. The dog was starting to get antsy, and the house felt odd without her presence. The little possum remained curled up on the afghan she had knitted for him, and grooming to calm himself, waiting.

Finally, the door opened and there she was – then she and the dog were gone. Aloysius crept out of his crate and went into the bathroom. With more determination than grace, he climbed over the ledge of the shower stall and arranged himself over the drain to pee.

By the time he was done, his human and the dog had come back inside. The possum watched as the dog stood still to have his feet wiped clean with a towel, the same way she dried him, although he didn't see her clean the dog's bottom.

Then she spotted him sitting on the rug in front of the shower.

"Aloysius!" she greeted him with undisguised delight. She swooped down on him, gathered him into her arms, and kissed him. A lot. He squirmed a bit, the familiar dizziness making him grip her hair with all the considerable strength in his hand.

"Let's lie down for just a minute," she suggested. "It was a long, long drive." Moving slowly so as not to exacerbate his disorientation, she laid down on the sofa with him still clutched to her chest. Keeping both hands on him lightly to help him balance, she petted his face. "You're all wet," she observed.

Gently she smoothed the fur by his eyes, making him close them. He was still sleepy, he decided, and laid his head down on her hand, and relaxed his whole body into her warm comfort. Before he fell asleep, he noticed her breathing slow and deepen.

Half an hour later, Aloysius woke, and lick-rubbed her hand until she woke as well. "Mmm, that was nice. You want to get down?" she asked, lifting him up and kneeling to set him carefully on the blanket on the floor. "Wow, it's late."

Lynda was already up, standing upright against the clear plexi barricade. Mom slid the barrier aside, letting Lynda loose. She ran into the room, paused on the blanket for a moment, then climbed onto the big wheel that Aloysius used, moving it at a pace he could never match. He watched from the side, unsure how to approach, clicking. He was ecstatic.

Mom went out to the kitchen.

"Cheese Night," Mom announced a few minutes later, and Lynda left the wheel to climb halfway up the woman's leg. Chuckling, Mom picked the tiny opossum up the rest of the way, tucked her casually into the crook of her arm, and carried her out to the kitchen, Aloysius keeping up as best he could.

By the time he got there, the dog had already taken up a position from which to watch for anything that fell (deliberate or accidental), and Lynda was way up on the counter, out of reach, smacking her way through a bowl of cheese cubes, chewing openmouthed with the most atrocious manners. Aloysius loved her.

Unable to reach Lynda, he settled for Mom, who was sitting on the floor, taking pictures of Lynda. Aloysius clicked, and lick-rubbed her free hand.

When Lynda announced she was done by knocking her dish to the floor, the woman gently disentangled Aloysius and stood. To his disappointment, she didn't put Lynda back on the floor, but took her to her room instead.

When she returned, she crouched down beside him and put a bowl of meunster cheese in front of him. The little opossum sniffed it over, then sat and waited. He was hungry.

With a quiet chuckle, Mom leaned over the top of him, bracing with one arm on either side, and fed him his dinner bite by bite, as he'd known she would.

Chapter 22

Footrubs

The little opossum loved his human, and lick-rubbed her at every opportunity to show her. Of course, he also lick-rubbed the hawk's ring perch, table legs, chair legs, corner of the cabinet, and various other spots around the house, but when he lick-rubbed her, he meant it with all his didelphic heart, and she knew it.

He often woke her up with a lick-rub, on whatever portion of her anatomy was closest or most convenient at the time. Usually it was her hands, if she was awake and petting him; if she was asleep, it might be her shoulder or head; but if she was sitting upright, distracted by typing (as happened more often now, in this new house) her feet were simply more accessible than anything else, frequently stretched straight to stick out on the other side of the short table she used.

To his pleased surprise, he had discovered that when he lick-rubbed her feet, she made small moaning noises, refrained from interrupting or disturbing him until he was well and truly done, and ran a running commentary: "Oh, my beloved little Aloysius, you give me more footrubs than any guy I've ever dated. And it feels … Oh. So. Good. Thank you, my love. You are so sweet to me, you utterly melt my heart. Mmm. I love you."

He loved the sound of her voice, and the praise and appreciation of such a simple act were heady ego boosts to the possum whose life she had saved. No, he had not forgotten. He would never forget how close he had been to death when he first came into her care.

Like many opossums, Aloysius could sometimes be enticed into a lickrub simply by the smell of fresh laundry, and he hadn't missed the fact that Mom made sure to always be wearing fresh footies, laced with the heady scent of fabric softener, in hopes of coaxing him into giving her the footrubs that gave her such exquisite physical as well as emotional pleasure.

Every night she changed footies at least once, sometimes two or three times in a single evening, blaming the dog for leaving puddles on the floor from his sloppy drinking (which he did), rainy weather, or even Charlie the starling for splashing water about in his bathtime excitement.

She claimed that she couldn't stand wearing wet footies, but Aloysius knew the truth was more complicated. Not only was she using fresh footies as bait, but on the off chance he was in a footrub sort of mood, she didn't want for him to have to lick-rub sullied footies.

He knew for an empirical fact that she really didn't mind if her feet were sopping wet and cold, because by the time he finished a lick-rub, his cheeks were generally plastered flat with saliva, and her fuzzy footies were soaked through and stuck to her skin – but she never, *ever* changed them right after a marsupial-spit-enhanced footrub, no matter how wet they were, or how chilly the evening.

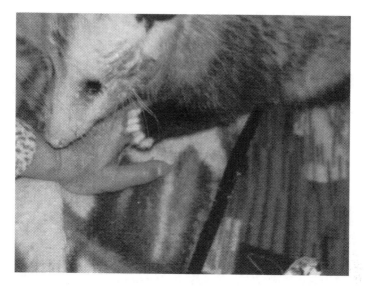

Chapter 23

Nutella

The eight-pound opossum butted his bearlike head against the side of his human's knee as she lay on her back. Immediately she woke, and cheerfully lifted both knees so he could stride beneath rather than walk all the way around her toes or awkwardly climb up over. He was very proud of her for her trainability, and knew she loved when he asked her to do things for him.

When he reached her other side, he stopped and thought for a moment, considering. Then he butted his head against her arm imperiously. It was 3:30 AM, and he was hungry. Well, he wanted a snack, anyway. Something better than the banana, almonds and grapes in the bowl by his water dish.

"What can I do for you, love?" Mom asked sleepily, sitting up and petting him. He butted her arm again. There was a jar of Nutella right there on the table, with the spoon. Come on.

"I suppose you could have some more Nutella," she said, as if coming up with this thought all on her own. She spooned out a small portion of the tantalizing treat, and let him scrape it off with his teeth. Aloysius chewed its sticky deliciousness with eyes half-closed in bliss, then looked for more.

"Maybe later, love," his human promised. "It really isn't good for you."

The opossum accepted this philosophically.

Cheese, some nice sliced Swiss cheese would be great right now, he thought. As if hearing this wish, she got up and walked out to the kitchen by the dim light of the nightlight. He followed her (with the dog trailing along behind, ready for handouts at any time of the day or night.)

She opened the cupboard and offered him a handful of dog kibble.

Really? He huffed and ignored it. If he'd wanted dog food, he would've rattled the dog's metal bowl.

Next, from the same cupboard, she produced a small dog biscuit, which he also occasionally liked, but not this time. He went toward the fridge as a sort of not-so-subtle hint.

Eager to please, she opened the fridge door and peered inside. Aloysius put one hand on the bottom by the drawer, and stretched his white snout upwards, sniffing in the direction of the cheese in what he considered a pretty blunt manner.

She opened the fruit bin, pulled a grape off the stem, rubbed it on her pajamas and offered it t him. He glanced at it in disbelief. A cold grape, really? She shrugged and ate it herself, then pulled out the leftover au gratin potatoes.

"How about some cheesy potatoes?" she asked, offering him the entire container. To think, just a scant few minutes ago he'd been proud of her intelligence. At least she was smart enough to correctly interpret his look of disdain, put the lid back on and return it to its shelf.

The little possum was starting to lose hope, when she pulled open the cheese drawer. Yes!

"You just had muenster for dinner, so you probably don't want more of that," she said. Like most of what she said to him, this seemed to require no reply, so he let it lay. "How about some Swiss?"

Aloysius brightened. Finally! He inhaled with pleasure as she unwrapped one delicious slice, ooking forward to accepting the first bite-size morsel ...

"Let's take it in on the blankets," she decided. Instead of eating yummy cheese, Aloysius found himself being transported dizzily to the other room and set down with infinite tenderness on the blanket.

"There you go," his human said, wrapping herself around him like a too-small t-shirt. Being a marsupial, he enjoyed the extreme proximity, and especially the dime-size piece of cheese she held in front of his nose.

Cocooned comfortably, he leaned against her arms to balance, and ate the entire slice bite by bite, chewing reverently while she kissed him, inhaled deeply of his fur, and mumbled soft endearments.

When the slice was gone, she showed him her empty hands, then wiped her fingers on her pajamas, and fell to petting him, stroking softly down his sides, and even gently caught his rose-petal ear between her lips, as he tried to wash up beneath such an onslaught of affection.

He put a small didelphic hand on one of her big human ones, gave her a quick back-and-forth headrub, and clicked. He loved her too, even if she wasn't as smart as a clever opossum.

Chapter 24

The New Sleeping-Spot

Aloysius hiked into the bathroom and curled up beside the toilet. His eight-pound marsupial self fit quite comfortably in the small cool space between the porcelain and the wall. It didn't bother him in the slightest that Mom came in periodically and there were loud watery noises afterwards. Quite the contrary, Aloysius derived a great deal of comfort and reassurance from her presence.

Every time she came in, even if just to wash her hands or toss some bit of fuzz or stray dead leaf in the bin beneath the sink, she always took the time to stop, and speak softly to him, and stroke his silken coat; and like any possum, Aloysius couldn't get enough of her attention and affection.

However, he couldn't help noticing that the floor in here wasn't as clean as the rest of the house. It wasn't exactly *dirty*, it just had hair on the floor. Not the dog's fluffy gold dust-bunnies, but her long human hair, dark brown, annoyingly ubiquitous and resilient.

He had to pull it out of his mouth after grooming, and he sometimes swallowed it. When that happened, it ended up in his poop, and sometimes he had to seek help from his human when he climbed out of the shower stall after a BM, and had the unsettling feeling of being followed. Fortunately nothing fazed her, and she could fix anything.

Tonight he had a weird feeling in his big toe on his left foot, the one that slid beneath him. Perhaps the mechanics of sliding on the floor caused two or three of his human's long hairs to roll around the end of his toe and twist, sinking in further than his teeth could catch, slowly cutting off circulation.

Well, this wasn't comfortable. Aloysius went in search of his human to fix this.

She sat on the floor on the blanket by the coffee table, typing on her laptop (which, despite its name, she never actually set on her lap.) The little possum hiked up to her and clicked at her.

"Aloysius!" she greeted him with undisguised delight. Computer forgotten, she picked up a dish of cheese and offered him some.

That wasn't what he'd come for. He needed her help. He ignored the cheese, but she didn't understand why.

In an effort to show her what was wrong, he sat back on his spine and licked his foot. Right in front of her, impossible for even a human to miss.

She frowned, then climbed right over the top of him, and peered close. "What's wrong with your toe, sweetie?"

She scooped him up, turned the bright overhead light on, and took him to the sofa. Turning him upside-down, she held him still and then looked at his foot, and tried to pull the twisted hairs off, but all she did was make it hurt. Aloysius squirmed. She didn't usually cause pain.

She said a Bad Word, turned the little possum right-side-up, and set him gingerly on the sofa. "I'll be right back," she promised.

He waited. He couldn't really do anything else; he wasn't able to get down off the sofa by himself. She came back within a minute, with a small sock, a piece of purple velcro, a tube of salve, and a small item that glinted in the light. She set it all on the coffee table, then gathered him up in her lap again, arranging him with his back to her chest, not quite upside-down, but not comfortable, either. She pulled her glasses off, and Aloysius knew that meant she was about to get close-up and personal.

He struggled, but she smooched his face and calmly reassured him that she loved him. He trusted her, and quieted, but his hand gripped the fingers of her left hand – the one holding his left foot – very tightly.

"You might need your nails clipped soon," was all she said, although he knew he was leaving marks.

She retrieved the small blade from the table, and bent her head over his foot. Suddenly there was a sharp pain in the already injured toe, and he couldn't help it, he twisted and bit her shoulder.

His bite went unacknowledged, as Mom carefully pulled the hairs from where they'd buried themselves deep in his toe. When she was sure they were gone, she put some white salve on, and the pain dimmed considerably. Fixed! So why wasn't she putting him on the floor?

Aloysius struggled once again as she slipped the sock over his foot, and wrapped the velcro strap around his ankle. Only then did she gently, carefully, set him on the floor.

"There you go, love. That's one of the socks Sara never got to use," she informed him. "I don't really expect you to keep it on, but even if it's just for a little while, it'll give the neosporin time to work."

Then she took the salve and knife out to the kitchen, and came back with a delicious piece of bologna, which she usually didn't let him have, claiming it was too salty and fatty and just plain not good. Aloysius begged to differ. It was very, very good, and he chewed in bliss.

Later he watched with approval as Mom scrubbed every inch of the bathroom floor with hot soapy water, and tossed the rugs in the washer.

Chapter 25

Mother's Day (with Lynda)

At about 4 AM, the eight-pound opossum decided it was time for breakfast. He circled around his sleeping human, finding just the right spot on her ribs, pressed his pointy white nose against her side, and *shoved*.

"Ah!" she yelped, waking instantly. Aloysius was gratified he'd gotten the exact spot right. Again.

Sniffing her hand with his quick, whistle-whispers, he clicked and lick-rubbed, dragging his head back and forth across her knuckles as she made happy little humming sounds.

After a minute or so, he realized she had gotten the camera and was video recording him. Well, at least videos didn't require bright flashes of light. He continued busily for another few seconds, then clicked again, and put his hand on her knee, looking up.

"Mmm, what a wonderful Mother's Day present! Thank you, my love," she murmured into the fur on top of his head, then kissed her way down the side of his face to his wet jawline. "Mmm, I love you."

Aloysius was all too aware this could easily devolve into a quarter-hour of inedible smooching. Turning on his twisted left leg, he led the way out to the kitchen, just in case she'd forgotten where it was. Humans, he'd learned, can act very peculiar when half asleep. (Not that being fully awake was any guarantee of coherent conduct.)

She opened the fridge and he patiently refused turkey, ham, eggs, and swiss cheese. Finally she produced more of the Muenster cheese he'd had for dinner, and he allowed her to feed it to him, one small cube at a time, with much gratuitous smooching.

When he couldn't eat another bite, he washed up, then she went to check on the girls.

Ziva! was first, and Aloysius lingered at the barricade to her room, clicking loudly as she ate her fruits and veggies while Mom cleaned her wheel. It always surprised Aloysius that the girls peed on their wheels, but he loved them nonetheless.

Nor did he understand Mom's difficulties getting in and out of Ziva!'s room with him there. He understood that the clear plexi had to be moved outwards, instead of sliding neatly to the side as the one at Lynda's door did, but did she really need him to back up halfway to the bathroom?

Sure, he saw Ziva! trying to get out at the same time he was trying to get in, while Mom was also trying to get through, but the plexi wouldn't actually hurt his fingers. It never had. Nor would Ziva! bite him; but Mom wasn't taking any chances.

At Lynda's door, Mom came to a full stop, aghast. "Oh, no, Lynda."

Lynda stood proudly at the doorway, both haunches plastered to her skin with dried poop. It had taken her a long time to get it just right; usually she was interrupted and Mom cleaned up anything in her potty pan. But sometimes, the interfering human slept too long, or didn't notice, and if the fit was on her, Lynda did her best to not smell like a tasty meal.

"Wow, that's quite a thorough job you've done of it," Mom commented with something akin to admiration. Lynda took it as a compliment. "But now you really, really need a bath."

She leaned over the barricade and Lynda stood upright, reaching toward her with her arms. The woman scooped her up – but instead of heading to the kitchen for treats, she took the little marsupial into the bathroom.

Aloysius tried to follow (he followed Mom everywhere, all the time) only to have the door shut rudely in his face! With typical possum patience, he settled in on the threshold to wait, clicking.

Lynda was neither patient, nor did she want to be in here. There was only one reason she was ever brought in the bathroom, and it wasn't fun. She wanted to get down, but Mom didn't let her, and then the shower was running. Lynda hated the shower.

Pulling the soft possum towel from a peg on the door, the woman made sure the temperature was right, then gently set Lynda on the shower floor. Hunching in a corner, Lynda suffered the wetting down, lathering up, and rinsing off process miserably.

A few times she tried climbing the woman's arms, but it didn't work, and she never got a chance at that braid she had successfully latched onto once. After what seemed like a long time (but was probably less than ten minutes) Mom shut off the water and towelled her as dry as a towel can get a furry soul.

She gathered the damp opossum into her arms, and inhaled approvingly. "Mmm, now you smell like raspberry shampoo," she said, opening the door.

Aloysius was overjoyed when Mom set Lynda on the floor again, following like the third in a game of follow-the-leader out into the kitchen. He loved Lynda however she smelled.

Mom opened the jar on the counter and took out three yummy treats. Handing one to Lynda, she said, "That was an interesting Mother's Day present, my little Lynda. I love you."

To Aloysius she just hummed a note and simply said, "I love you."

Then she went to Ziva!'s room, and called. Ziva! dug her way out of her sleeping hut, and ran to the barricade. "Ziva!," Mom greeted her, picking her up and feeding her the last treat. "Happy Mother's Day, love." She set the little possum back in her room while she was still chewing.

Scooping up Lynda, she returned her to her room as well, latching the barricade.

Then she turned to Aloysius, sat on the blanket on the floor, and tenderly pulled him into her lap. Then she leaned back as he expected, and he moved to stand on her chest, sniffing her face. He loved his silly human. He rubbed his pink nose back and forth across her smiling lips and clicked.

"Mmmm! Oh, Aloysius, this is the best Mother's Day in my entire life." She raised her head and kissed him reverently between his rose-petal ears.

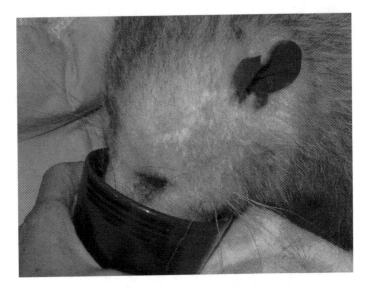

Chapter 26

Tea on the Deck

Mom smooched his head and shoulders as he lick-rubbed the back of her hand, then he made to walk over her arm and check out the kitchen.

She gently dragged him back, continuing to kiss him, and Aloysius gripped her fingers with his hand and licked her knuckles again, completely forgetting he'd been about to leave.

"Gaaaah!" Mom suddenly straightened up. "Whisker up by doze, at least four idches logg." She sat there, her hand to her nose, blinking rapidly. Aloysius had no idea what she just said. English was slippery at best, but this was complete gibberish.

"It's OK, I'm OK," she said, hunkering down once again. Before she got even one real smooch in, she gave him a hasty kiss on the head. "Oh, no, my tea!" She leaped up and was out the door.

The small opossum was left to stare after her in bewilderment. She had gone out the side door, so she probably wasn't going to work, which meant she'd probably be back soon.

Sure enough, she was. She put a cup in the microwave, left it humming electronically, and gathered up a blanket and a book.

Crouching down in front of Aloysius with her arms full, she asked, "How about going out on the deck for a little while? It's beautiful out!" Without waiting for a reply, she pressed another kiss to the top of his head, and was gone again. It was just as well; Aloysius had no answer she'd want to hear. Beautiful out, indeed. He resigned himself to another session of "enjoying" the Great Outdoors.

Sure enough, Mom came back in empty handed, and gently, tenderly, scooped him up and hauled him out onto the wooden deck. There was a railing around it, and she sat on a blanket leaning up against the side of the house, with the small marsupial in her lap. The sun was shining, and there was birdsong all around them, much louder and clearer than he was used to hearing it through the walls.

"You want some tea?" his human asked.

Aloysius gave it a cursory sniff, and politely declined. There was way too much to see and hear for him to want to stick his head inside a teacup and slurp.

"What's wrong with it? You love tea," she worried.

He gave her knuckles a quick lick and a brief backwards rub of his head to reassure her, and she scooched her knees up so he could wedge his bottom against them, and apply himself to a real lick-rub of both her hands, employing lots of spit.

Only when his head-fur stood up in rakish tufts and the sleeves of her pajamas were plastered to her arms did he stop. (It was mid-afternoon and the woman was still in pajamas. Some days she didn't get out of pajamas until evening, when she showered and put on fresh pajamas.)

With his nose angled up to catch the light breeze, he slid off Mom's lap and stood, unsteady and uncertain, on the blanket he recognized from Ziva!'s room. He took stock of his surroundings. The big dog sprawled in the sun a few feet away, and there was also a cat, temporarily inoffensive in a midday doze.

There were interesting scents here, and Aloysius was intrigued in spite of himself. He made his way to the edge of the blanket, then balked. Distrustful, he smelled the painted wood of the deck, then realized this whole thing was a really dumb idea and he really wanted to be back inside now, right NOW. He skittered backwards until he felt Mom's reassuring bulk against his butt, her hands on his sides helping keep him upright.

"Sweetie, have you had enough of being outside?" she asked, concern and love palpable in her voice.

He turned and pressed his face to the side of her leg in a brief, lickless rub of assent.

Thankfully she got the hint, and never was he so glad to be picked up. Leaving everything else out there, she carried him back inside, the screen door shutting behind them with a metallic clang that sounded like relief to the little possum.

Mom settled him in the down comforter by his travel crate and gave him a piece of banana cookie, then went to bring in the stuff off the deck, including the fuzzy dog. When she came back in, she re-reheated her tea, and offered it to Aloysius again.

This time he lapped happily at the sweet, creamy concoction, getting it all over his face and Mom. She laughed and kissed a droplet off the top of his nose while he tried to lick-rub her hand holding the teacup, almost setting them both awash in sticky tea.

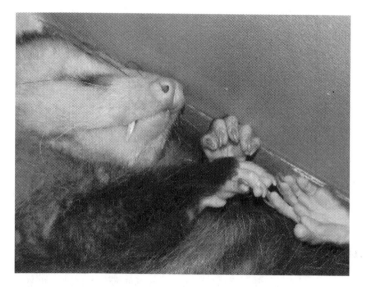

Chapter 27

Sleepover in Lynda's Library

Aloysius woke from his midday slumber to toddle out and see what mom was up to. She was home during daylight hours, which was unusual. She sat crosslegged in front of her laptop, easily accessible, and he climbed up on her lap to lick-rub her proffered hand. The house smelled different today; several windows were open, and enough warm breeze came in that the big fan on the ceiling moved slowly, silently overhead. The little opossum ignored it.

On his way to his water bowl for a drink, he noticed that the barricade to Lynda's room was wide open! Cheerfully he wandered in, took a drink from her water bowl instead, and looked around, clicking. He could smell her female self, all over everything in the place. It was intoxicating.

First, he investigated her wheel, sniffing at the paper towels with close interest. He put one hand on the curve of the walking surface, but it was uncomfortably high – maybe three inches from the floor – and he decided not to try climbing up on.

Next he sniffed at her potty pan, then decisively squatted and marked it as *his*. Mom (who was hovering throughout his exploration) patted him dry with a tissue, then stepped back and let him continue.

Clicking loudly, he searched for Lynda, but couldn't find her, although he knew she had to be close by. She didn't respond to his clicks, but he didn't expect her to.

He walked over the end of a sleeping bag with a teddy bear tucked into the opening, gave it a few lick-rubs, then sallied behind an ornate wooden magazine rack.

Well, that looked like fun to lick-rub! Aloysius braced his unsteady self on the uncertain surface of a folded down comforter, and gave one decorative wagon wheel a lick-rub. The effort overbalanced him, and he fell onto his side, unable to right himself trapped in the valley between the blanket and the wall.

Mom was immediately there, tenderly lifting him up and setting him on his feet again. Aloysius licked her hand in thanks, then resumed his interrupted lick-rub of the magazine rack, gripping the thing in one fist to maintain his dicey balance.

When his cheeks were wet and he was satisfied, he moved on to the tall bookshelf. Some of the books on the lower shelf smelled of Lynda, and he gave them a nibble or two, before he discovered the narrow cranny between the side of the bookshelf and the wall. What a great sleeping-spot! He walked in, curled up and started to groom himself.

"You want some dog kibble?" His human fished several yummy pieces from a bowl on a shelf, and fed them to Aloysius one by one, as he lay on his back in the narrow nook. He crunched with pleasure, his eyes closed, simply expecting the next piece to be there when he was ready. When he heard her wipe her hands on her jeans then felt her pet him while he chewed, he knew that one was the last.

Ah, but she had a surprise for him. "You never ate your banana," she said, kneeling down with a bowl in her hand. A luscious half-slice of banana appeared before his pink heart-shaped nose.

Banana? What a great idea for dessert! Aloysius took the sticky treat in his mouth, careful as always of Mom's fingers, and smacked his way through the piece of fruit. One by one he polished off the bowlful, until the woman showed him the empty bowl, and set it aside.

With her clean hand, she stroked his fur, and he included her fingers in his post-prandial washup, making her chuckle.

"You are so sweet to me, Aloysius," she told him, as she'd told him a hundred times before. She couldn't quite get her face in his cramped sleeping quarters, so she settled for kissing her fingers and brushing them over the top of his head.

"Go to sleep, love, I'll be here when you need to get out of there," she promised.

Hours later, when he tried to turn around, he found the comfy little nook a bit too confining, and he scrabbled on the wall, unable to stand. Sure enough, in moments Mom was there, picking him up and holding him to her until he calmed down.

She might have held him a trifle longer than strictly necessary, but Aloysius did't mind. When she put him down, he chose to finish his nap in Lynda's crate, relaxing into the crocheted afghan with drowsy pleasure, as his human petted his silky self. It was a good day.

Chapter 28

Bewits, Bells, and Blueberry Muffin

Hearing activity in the kitchen, the little opossum side-stepped his way out to see if he could cadge treats. His human always dropped whatever she was doing to greet him, and she was delighted out of all proportion when he ate goodies from her fingers. He wondered what treats she had for him tonight.

He clicked, and pressed himself between her ankles and the cabinets, standing on her fuzzy-sock-clad feet. She loved when he stood on her feet. In point of fact, she often didn't even know he was there until she felt him.

"Aloysius!" came the expected happy reaction, and she petted his sides until he stepped off her feet, then she knelt and enwrapped the small opossum in her arms with unfeigned delight. He clicked again, and held her hand with his smaller, but stronger one for a brief lick-rub. (He knew he was stronger because she always had to wait for him to let go when he held her, but he easily escaped her when he wanted to.)

But the purpose of this visit wasn't really all hugs and kisses. He had just woken up, and he was hungry. What delectable dishes was she serving for dinner tonight? He could smell cheese, and various fruits.

"It's Cheese Night," Mom informed him, offering a cube of Meunster.

Aloysius sniffed it dismissively. What else was there?

One by one his human offered various items from the fridge without success, until Aloysius' fingers and toes started feeling chilled from standing in front of the open door. Wasn't there anything possum-worthy in there?

His nose twitched as she opened a plastic bag. What was that heavenly scent? It was kind of like those tart frozen blueberries she occasionally put in his fruit salad as obstacles to the grapes and banana, but this also had the delicious aroma of the cinnamon rolls she hardly shared any of.

"This isn't even vaguely nutritional," Mom informed him, breaking off a piece. "But, do you want some blueberry muffin?" She held the piece in front of his nose, and Aloysius went stock-still for a moment in pure delirious disbelief.

He engulfed the treat and her fingers in his mouth, closing down enough to hold onto the savory sweet fluffy food while allowing Mom to reclaim her fingers unscathed by his razor-sharp teeth. Then he settled in to extract as much pleasure as possible from the mouthful of ambrosia. It was cool from the fridge, and the sweetness made him salivate. He squinted his eyes and concentrated on not losing a single drop.

When he finished, another piece was waiting in front of him, and he accepted it with relish. Several pieces later, Mom wrapped up what was left and put it back in the fridge.

"You won't have room for anything substantial if you fill up on goodies," she chided him. He knew she was desperate when she brought out the cream cheese.

Fingerful by fingerful, Aloysius slurped the soft cheese from Mom's fingers, until finally he was full. He drew back and braced against her arms to wash up, then tottered off toward the dog's water dish. At this time of the evening, it should still be relatively drool-free.

"Hey sweetie, look at this," the woman said, holding an item up for his inspection. "It's a bell, on a bewit."

Intrigued, Aloysius took it from her in one little fist and sniffed it over. It was just a small strip of leather that smelled of oil, and a metal sphere that jingled when it moved. Ah, but the leather smelled *soooo* good! He pressed it to the floor and lick-rubbed it, biting at it periodically for good measure.

As she often did when he had hold of something interesting, Mom brought out the camera. He had vast experience ignoring the bright flashes, and continued as if she weren't there. This bewit had a trace of the same birdscent that he loved so much on the ring-perch, and he drooled and rubbed and bit until finally there was a puddle of possum spit on the floor, and the sides of his face were drenched with it.

Finally coming up for air, he dropped the bit of leather with a musical jingle, recalled his surroundings, and hiked toward his own little bowl of water for a good, long drink. He retreated to his den beneath the drafting desk to wash up, as Mom picked up the bell and wiped the floor dry.

Then she came over to the desk and contorted herself to kiss the top of his head. "I love you, Aloysius, and I love when I find something you enjoy. We'll see what else is in the box of hawk stuff that's safe for you to have."

Aloysius licked her hand and clicked. He loved new things to play with and investigate, but most of all, he loved *her.*

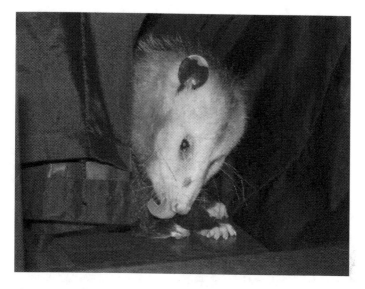

Chapter 29

Aloysius Finds a New Hiding Spot

"Aloysius?" the woman called. "Aloysius. I've got cheese," she wheedled. "Where are you, love?"

The eight-pound opossum cleaned the fingernails of his left hand, unconcerned. She'd find him. She always did. The house really wasn't that big, and two rooms were barricaded off for the girls. But for now he chose to enjoy his rare moment of solitude.

He'd been lick-rubbing the metal legs of the kitchen table when he noticed this dark little nook. The woman's black raincoat draped over the back of one of the chairs created a three-quarter semicircle just the right size for a small marsupial, and the base of the chair gave him a comfortably rounded plastic angle to brace his uncoordinated self against. Really, it was perfect.

That Mom couldn't find him was merely icing on the cake.

"Aloysius!" Uncertainty and panic had crept into her voice.

Taking pity on her at last, Aloysius turned to groom his left flank, which made his tail slip out from under the back of the coat.

In a few minutes, he heard a sharp intake of breath, then a flashlight shone on his hands (but not in his eyes; she was considerate, and he appreciated that) and he calmly returned the gaze of his human, his savior and protector and servant.

"There you are," she said, stating the obvious, more upset than he'd realized.

He clicked at her. Clicking always made her happy, and this time was no exception.

At the sound she smiled. "I love your clicks." Then she disappeared.

Aloysius knew from experience that if she caught him doing something interesting and then suddenly left, it was probably to fetch up the camera.

Sure enough, when she came back, the familiar bright flash temporarily blinded his nocturnal eyes. He mentally shrugged, and climbed over one chair leg to go lick-rub her hands. With luck, she might invite him out to the kitchen for some sort of treat.

Instead, he felt himself being lifted dizzily off his feet and clutched tightly to her. She'd apparently been really upset.

"I love you, Aloysius, and need you," she reminded him. Again. Carrying him out to the kitchen (which he recognized as a flimsy excuse for picking him up) she fished around in the fridge, finally coming up with a silver-wrapped brick.

"How about some cream cheese?" she asked, spooning out a delicious bite and offering it to him in her fingers.

Well, for cream cheese he'd forgive her for lifting him off his precarious footing. He smacked appreciatively and looked for the next bite, which of course she had ready and waiting for him. After several bites, she stood, put the cheese away and washed her fingers.

She crouched low to kiss him and then wandered back to the living room.

Following her, Aloysius noticed that Lynda was awake and begging for treats and attention, and Mom was about to go in her room. The little male possum humbly asked if he could go in and see Lynda, too, but Mom wouldn't let him.

"I'm just going to be a minute, love," she told him.

Aloysius waited right outside the barricade.

To his delight, when she came back out she had Lynda's travel crate with her. "Here, love, I know you like sleeping in her crate, even though I can't let you spend the day in her room when I'm at work."

She set the crate down near her blanket, and neatened the afghan inside.

Aloysius clicked and sniffed the afghan with approval. Lynda had been inside since the last time he'd slept there. Mmmm, the smell of her was yummy. He went inside and awkwardly lick-rubbed the side of crate, cramped by the small space and hampered by his own balance difficulties, but ecstatic nevertheless.

He peered out and caught Mom smiling at him. She loved doing things for him, and he loved her for it. Unsteadily he made his way out of the crate and over to her. As expected, she leaned down to kiss him, and the little possum reached up and rubbed his nose along her lips in a patented possum-kiss.

Chapter 30

Aloysius Goes to the Vet

It didn't take a genius opossum to know something was terribly wrong.

Although it was nearly three in the morning, he'd had nothing to eat since before midnight. No little plate of fruits and veggies waited for him on his placemat, and she'd even forgotten to give him water! Finally desperate enough to drink from the dog's drooly ceramic dish, he was dismayed when he couldn't find it.

Similarly, the dog's metal dinner bowl was missing. How was he supposed to announce his desire for treats if he couldn't bang the dog bowl around?

Hoping for handouts, the small opossum walked in circles around his human as she sat on the floor in front of her computer, but she just petted him, and each time he climbed up onto her lap, she merely hugged him and kissed him, as if she didn't understand that he was starving.

Had she decided to quit feeding him? She seemed to still love him, but he needed to eat and drink, too! His only consolation was that she wasn't eating, either, although she usually had some sort of snack when he got her up at this hour.

"It's only another few hours," she assured him. "I'll bring cheese and grapes along so you can have something as soon as you're awake afterwards."

Awake after what? He was awake now, and hungry! But she could not be cajoled into even the smallest nibble. She just assured him she loved him, and showered him with kisses and hugs too numerous to count. As dawn lightened the sky outside, Aloysius gave up and crept into his crate-den, dejected, and tried to sleep despite his empty stomach.

He had just drifted off when his human put the barred door on the front of his crate, petted him softly, then locked him in. Well, that couldn't be good. She carried him, crate and all, to the car.

It was a long trip, almost half an hour, which Aloysius spent alert and anxious. When they stopped, Mom carried his crate into a building he'd never been in, but he recognized it well enough. Noplace else smells like a veterinarian's office.

They waited a short time in the front room with a yappy little dog, then moved into a private exam room. Soon a very nice man gently but thoroughly looked him over, admired his teeth, and then picked up a small syringe.

"Usually I'd have one of my techs hold him for this, but I don't want them near him until he's out," the vet said. "Hold his head as if his life depends on it. If he bites anybody, we won't need x-rays."

Always before Mom had handled Aloysius gently, tenderly; but now at the behest of this man, she overpowered him, pinning his head immobile to the cold table. Aloysius struggled, then felt a sharp sting in his haunch, and suddenly Mom let go of his head and gathered him up in her arms, kissing his head and face.

The vet voiced his disapproval of this risky behavior, but the woman ignored his dire warnings.

"I'm so sorry, love, so so sorry." Aloysius could tell she was on the verge of tears, and wanted to reach up to run his nose along her lips – but he felt overwhelmingly sleepy. Giving a deep sigh from the very soles of his feet, he melted into her embrace. The last thing he knew was mom kissing the big freckle on his nose.

Consciousness had returned some time ago, but Aloysius was feeling very much in the mood for comfort and petting, which his human always provided in excess. Now he basked in it, laying quite comfortably along her legs, his head in the palm of her hand exactly the way he liked best.

Her free hand stroked him gently, reverently, from head to hip, the rhythm slow and soothing and somniferous. He drowsed, and time didn't matter.

Eventually the door opened, and the little possum heard the deep tones of the veterinarian. "How's he doing?" Accustomed to his human servant's deference, Aloysius was entirely unprepared for the big hand that casually ruffled through his fur the way Mom petted the big retriever. Well, that wasn't very restful. Aloysius stood, and shook, and gave a big yawn.

"Ha, the drug wore off long ago, he's just been sleeping," the vet cheerfully accused, as if sleeping were some sort of crime. He pronounced them good to go.

Gladly Mom slid Aloysius backwards into his crate, set a handful of grapes and cheese cubes in front of his nose, and they returned to the car. Aloysius had no idea how long it took to drive home; he fell asleep again as soon as the snacks were gone.

When he woke, it was full dark, and everything was as it should be: his own water bowl, clean and fresh; a dish of fruit salad, and a bowl of scrambled egg. He ate the egg, snubbed the fruit, and walked up to Mom. She greeted him with a spoonful of Nutella, and all was right with the world.

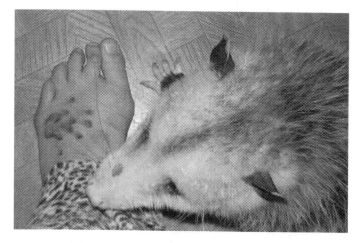

Chapter 31

Aloysius's Handprint on Mom's Foot

It began when Aloysius wasn't even awake. Mom had gone online, made a phone call, and then came over to where the little opossum was sleeping in his crate on his ultra-soft afghan. She fed him two mouse tails, which Aloysius chewed with bliss, then she kissed her fingers and touched them to his head. (She couldn't quite reach to kiss him conventionally; she tried.)

"I'll be back, my love, and wait till you see what I'm going to get," she murmured excitedly. "I love you."

Then she left.

Hours later she returned, absolutely jubilant. "Aloysius, look!" she said, toeing out of her sneakers and pulling off her socks.

There, on top of her left foot, was a shaded lilac version of Aloysius's own right handprint. So this was why she had gotten ink all over his hand and pressed it to paper the other day.

Well, he was glad she was happy, because he loved her, of course, and because it usually meant snacks and smooching. Aloysius snickered to himself. As opposed to when she was upset, which generally meant snacks and smooching. He walked up and over her foot right across the handprint, ignoring her attempts to take a photo of the momentous event.

She put her fuzzy footies back on, and proceeded to divvy up cheese and fruits and veggies. Not that Aloysius ever actually ate any of the veggies; sometimes he wouldn't even eat the fruit, unless Mom handed it to him one bite-size piece at a time. She really was a wonderfully well-trained human.

And he did love her and appreciate her, and tried to let her know as often as he could. Now he walked in tight circles around her feet, as always with the left side of his body pressed against her ankles, leaning on her to keep his balance as his painful leg slid underneath him.

A piece of Velveeta appeared in front of his nose, and he stopped walking to take both it and the woman's fingers into his wide, dagger-filled mouth, carefully working the delicious cheese out from between her fingers, his razor-sharp teeth not leaving so much as a scratch, he was so gentle.

He chewed thoughtfully, and then refused the next piece.

"But you love Velveeta," Mom assured him.

That was *yesterday*, Aloysius said to himself. He gripped her pajama leg with one hand and looked up, sniffing hopefully. This was a ploy that he knew she was unable to resist.

She turned toward the refrigerator, but when she pulled her foot out from under him, her footie caught on one of his fangs. He was almost a year old, and his heavy saber teeth extended a good half-inch below his jawline. Luckily she moved slowly around him; as it was, his head was yanked several inches before she froze and disentangled him.

"Are you okay, sweetie?" she asked, crouching and feeling his fangs. When she reassured herself that he was intact, she opened the fridge door and pulled out a flat triangular item.

Unwrapping the plastic from around it, she scooched down to hunch over him, with one elbow on either side of his shoulders, and then peeled a mouthful of tomato-sauce-flavored mozzarella cheese from the top of the pizza for him, kissing the top of his head as she did.

Aloysius accepted it as if doing her a favor by accepting, but it was good and he enjoyed it immensely. Bit by bit she handed him pieces of cheese, and even some tiny fragments of pepperoni, but he noticed she ate most of that herself.

The dog, no dummy, smelled what was going on and laid down with feigned disinterest a few feet away. He was too well-bred to beg, but he could and did use ruthless, patient proximity with real talent.

As each section of crust was stripped, the woman slid it across the floor to the dog, who obligingly cleaned up, helping keep the place tidy. What a trooper.

After the last bite of pizza cheese, Aloysius took some time to masticate and press the fibrous bread dough he had unintentionally eaten along with the luscious cheese, finally spitting out a crescent-shaped spat. Then, bracing against Mom's arms, he carefully washed his face and hands, and Mom's hands too, because he was just that polite.

Chapter 32

Vet Visit Redux

Once again, Aloysius woke to Mom putting the wire door on his travel crate early in the morning, and once again she had refused all his best efforts to cadge treats from two o'clock on. Something was up, and the little possum knew it wasn't going to be good.

A half-hour drive and yep, they were back at the vet's. Mom opened his crate and kissed and petted him, assured him she would stay right there and not leave him, and invited the nice vet tech to also pet him. Well, Aloysius never objected to affection in his life, and only rarely did his human allow other humans to pet him, so he sniffed Betsy politely and enjoyed her gentle touch.

Then his crate was closed and he was taken away from Mom. He felt bad for leaving her. Who would stand on her feet? But he had to pay attention to all the new sights and smells and sounds. There were dogs and cats, and a large bird with a huge heavy beak screeching at top decibels. He was taken past all these, to a big open room with stainless steel tables.

His crate was taken apart and calm, confident hands picked him up and held him, another person did something, and then it was just too much effort to stay awake. Aloysius fell asleep.

When he woke, he was immensely relieved to find Mom wrapped around him where he lay in an open metal cage. Drowsily he reached with his hand to grasp her fingers, and licked her knuckles as she kissed his face over and over, murmuring that she loved him, and that this should make him feel better.

Now that he thought about it, the sharp grinding pain was gone from his left hip. There was a deep achy soreness there, but nothing like the pain he'd resolutely grown accustomed to. He struggled to sit up, but Mom gently held him down, and he almost immediately gave up. He was completely exhausted, although he couldn't remember doing anything to get that way.

A vet tech came over and took his temperature in a decidedly impolite manner, vanished, then returned with a heating pad and a bag of warm cracked corn. After sliding the heating pad beneath the towel he lay on, then settling the warm bag against the length of his body, she counted his pulse and respiration, then left again.

Every fifteen minutes someone came and monitored his temperature, then rearranged or re-heated the corn bag. "It has to stay between 94 and 96," the tech told Mom, when the small device once again failed to reach a satisfactory reading.

Finally, after slightly over two hours, he was allowed an entire half hour before another monitoring session. He licked Mom's hands yet again, and shifted to fall against her arm, pressing himself up against her familiar, comforting presence.

When the intrusive thermometer gave a happy reading for the third time in a row, the veterinarian came to sit with them and talk to Mom while she held him. He was quite cheerful and pleasant, and Aloysius liked him, although he didn't remember any of what the doctor was telling Mom.

He spoke of cutting the femoral head back, and padding the false joint with a fatty layer. Aloysius moved to stand again, feeling stronger and wanting to go home. He was incredibly thirsty, and there seemed to be no water bowls set out at convenient spots for a possum here.

Eventually, Mom gently slid him in his familiar blessed crate-den, with his very own afghan knitted by his very own human. After a deceptively brief transaction at the counter, Mom promised to bring him back yet again on the third, but for now they were free to go, and she took him out into the sunshine to the car.

When they got home, Aloysius availed himself of the dog's water bowl, and drank blissfully. Then he tottered into the bathroom and curled up next to the toilet. Mom disappeared, and then returned with macaroni and cheese! Aloysius ate his fill, bite by bite, and then he slept long and deeply. Peripherally he was aware of Mom checking on him every so often, and she too was rather impolite with a thermometer.

About an hour later, after yet another temperature check, he felt her hands sliding beneath his body as she lifted him up and held him close to her. "You're too cold here, my love," she explained. "How would you like to go sleep in Lynda's crate? She won't mind, she's in her sleeping bag," Mom murmured into his silky ear. His ears still had pink edging along their tops, although today (Mom assured him) he was officially one year old.

The small possum didn't object as she carried him into, not out of, Lynda's room! Then she carefully placed him inside Lynda's doorless crate. Aloysius clicked, softly and drowsily, at the heavenly scent of Lynda all around him, and fell into happy dreams. His human took his temperature a couple more times, but he didn't bother waking up for it.

By three AM, Aloysius was feeling much more alert and energetic, and he sallied out in search of good things to eat. Mom heard him moving around, and hastened to undo the barricade. The ache was still there inside his hip, but it was nothing like the pain he'd become accustomed to.

"What can I get you, love? You want some mouse tails?" she asked. Leaving him alone on the blanket by Lynda's room, she rummaged around in the freezer, then Aloysius heard scissors. Shortly Mom came back, with three luscious mouse tails! They were still frozen, but he didn't mind.

Huddling over him like a mother hen, she then plied him with grapes, and banana cookie, bologna, and finally a tiny bit of Nutella on the top of a teaspoon. Oh! How wonderful. Aloysius scooched backwards in her embrace until he wedged himself fairly sturdily, then proceeded to wash up.

Finally he felt sleepy enough to seek out his den. His human accompanied him as she had all night, laying out a blanket next to his crate to sleep on, so she could have an arm inside his crate with him.

Aloysius actually liked when she did this; he licked her hand and arm, and then flopped over onto his side against her warm reassuring solidity. He gave a deep sigh of contentment.

"Sweetie?" Mom asked, her voice uncertain, worried. "You never banged the dog dish tonight."

Aloysius roused enough to lick-rub her hand once, then lay his head down in her palm. When had he had a moment alone tonight? He only banged the dog bowl around to get her attention, and she had been focused intently on him constantly, showering him with goodies. Ah, humans.

The next night he was up at his normal time, and even Mom commented on how extra affectionate he was. He waited until she was doing something on the computer, then he banged the dog bowl around and waited.

Her reaction was highly gratifying. She immediately leaped up and came over to crouch over him on the floor. "You banged on the dog dish," she said, amazed. Aloysius could hear incipient tears in her voice, so he took her hand in his own smaller one, and gave her a quick lick-rub.

That just seemed to make it worse. She started crying, but that didn't stop her from getting up and bringing back a plastic bag from the freezer, full of mouse tails!

One by one she handed them to him while laughing and crying at the same time, and Aloysius knew he was loved.

Chapter 33

Aloysius Receives a Gift Box in the Mail

Aloysius, like Mom, looked up when the dog barked. It wasn't the retriever's usual vague "somebody somewhere, or maybe a dog barking" woof; this was a thunderous salvo meant to warn an imminent visitor that a large dog stood ready to defend this house and family. Sure enough, as Mom gently moved Aloysius from her lap to the floor, a knock came at the door.

"Arth," his human said, calm and quiet as she stood, laid a hand on the dog's head like a benediction, and went to the door. The dog gave one more soft woof, then sighed and laid down, accepting that the woman had the situation under control.

Hah! Aloysius knew better. It was into rose-petal possum ears that she whispered her fears and weaknesses, wishes and heartbreaks. For the dog she feigned a confident veneer. This visitor might be intent on mayhem, who knew? The small opossum shifted his stance to peer around the edge of the sofa as Mom spoke briefly with a uniformed man.

The man handed her a box, and turned away; Aloysius heard the truck start up and drive off, as Mom shut the door and brought the box in to lay it on the floor in front of him. Happy wonder shone in her eyes.

"Aloysius, it's for *you*," she said, bending down to smooch his head. She went to the kitchen and came back with a small knife, which she used to carefully open the box.

Inside he could smell an interesting assortment of food.

Mom picked him up and set him on the sofa. Ah, a photo session. Aloysius drew a resigned didelphic sigh from the depths of his diaphragm, and as was his wont, made the best of it.

"It's all goodies to go with tea!" Mom proclaimed, and Aloysius pricked up his pink-edged ears. He liked tea; or rather, he liked warm, sweetened heavy cream, which was what Mom's tea really was. Maybe this would prove to be a fun time in spite of the repeated camera flash.

Soon he was surrounded by edible oddities, which Mom opened and offered to him. First there were the tiny cookies, which smelled good enough for him to accept one, but once it was in his mouth it felt and tasted peculiar, so he spit it out.

"You don't like it? That's OK, don't worry, Lynda or Ziva! will eat it," Mom said, setting it aside. Really, he hadn't been worrying.

"Try this, it's mmmm, excellent." She offered him a piece of what appeared to be wafer with some sort of filling. When he refused it, she didn't insist, and ate it herself.

The possum poked his bearlike nose into the mug, hoping despite the lack of yummy tea-scent that it at least might prove edible. Nope, empty. He sneezed his disappointment. Next came a bag of hard sugary things. Aloysius was all for sweet stuff, but these things had an odd tannic taste, mixed with lemon. Humans *liked* these? He turned his head sharply away.

"This is just tea," his human said, showing him two unopened packages. Tea? This stuff was dry and had not a whiff of heavy cream.

"And I don't think you'd like rock candy," she said, starting to pick up the items around him, putting them back in their excelsior packing. Was there nothing worth eating in this entire box? He leaned on the sofa arm and sniffed the air.

"Hang on," she said, stooping to brush a light smooch on the top of his head. She took the box of things out to the kitchen, and he heard the freezer door open and close. He leaned his elbows on the sofa arm in mute hope, but he knew better than to risk his dicey balance by actually climbing up.

Only about one time in ten did the sound of the freezer door herald that most delicious of snacks: mouse tails. But right now his human was aware of his disappointment in these exotic comestibles, and just might be inclined to produce something actually tasty.

He heard the promising sound of plastic rattling, and pulled himself a bit farther up onto the sofa arm.

Here she came, with an indulgent smile and something in her hand. Scooping him up off his unsteady perch, she sat crosslegged on the floor and held him half on his back, tucked up against her warm body.

And there, in front of his nose, appeared a mouse tail. Eagerly he grabbed at her hand with his own, and engulfed the tail and two of her fingers in his mouthful of daggers. Carefully extracting the frozen tail without so much as scratching her skin, Aloysius chewed in bliss, crunching happily at the bones.

Now *this* was a treat. He ate all she had brought for him, then carefully washed up, generously including her fingers in his ministrations. Life was good.

Louise

Every evening when she woke up, Louise thoroughly washed her face and hands and ears, then her whole entire self, for a good half hour before sauntering out with the happy hip-swing pace of complacency that opossums have used for millennia.

Often her first order of the night was exercise. Louise loved her go-round toy, even though she was a full-grown opossum now, and had long ago outgrown being able to use the small exercise wheel as she did when she was small enough to fit. Instead, now she stood upright beside the thing, using her strong and supple tail to balance, and she played a hand-over-hand sort of game with the wheel, to the delight of her adoring human.

Louise wasn't always big and strong and healthy. When she first came to live with her human Mom, she weighed barely four-and-a-half ounces, and it was a long time before she could be allowed free run of the house. But love and heroic effort prevailed, and Louise not only survived, she thrived, and soon considered the house, and especially the doting human, hers.

She took her responsibilities seriously, and did her best to supervise the most important of her human's decisions (especially what to fix for dinner.) So of course when Mom decided to remodel the bathroom, Louise was there to help.

One Monday, a stranger came to the door. Louise ambled in that direction with her patient but purposeful possum stride from the den and through the sunroom in the back of the house, while the two cats raced each other to the front door.

Mom gently pushed the cats aside. "Sit, and stay," she said, because no one had ever told her that cats can't be trained like dogs.

Lancelot and Merlin sat and stayed, because they hadn't been told, either.

The man and Mom discussed how best to get the new glass shower door inside. Mom agreed that the front entrance would be fine, but pointed at the cats. "Bring it through here, just don't let the cats–"

She stopped, noticing that now there was one cat, a possum, and then another cat watching this exchange. Mom tenderly scooped up the marsupial. "And do not step on Louise."

"I've never seen anything like that," the man said.

"I don't know where you're from, but around here we call them possums," Mom replied.

The man chuckled. "I know what they are, I've just never seen one running around a house with two cats."

Louise's human explained to the man how peaceful opossums are, that Louise loved children and even the dogs that came to visit, and let him pet her and feel how soft her fur was. Louise quickly and easily added another fan for opossums everywhere, all before breakfast.

Sometimes her human took her outside just to sit in the sunshine, and while Louise enjoyed all the new smells and sounds and sights, she was glad that Mom was always right there, and that they didn't stay out long. It was usually hot outside, and snacks were few and far between.

Photo by Rachael Howard

Better were the days she got to accompany her human to church. Sometimes Mom simply sat at the courtesy desk for several hours, and Louise happily greeted guests or napped. She also occasionally attended church meetings, and was so well-mannered that many of the humans didn't even knew she was there.

Most of the members of the large church knew of her, however, and she was welcomed with genuine pleasure at various church functions, including the Trunk-Or-Treat celebration for children in October, for which she had two different outfits. This takes place outside in the church's parking lot at a pleasantly cool time of year, and Louise enjoyed her celebrity status and the fresh air from the comfort of Mom's lap.

Graciously Louise allowed children and adults alike to admire her, teaching them how valuable opossums are to the ecosystem. She wasn't able to survive in the wild and contribute to her species by making joeys, but she did a great job of PR for her wild cousins.

Glenn of Lime Hollow (used with permission)

Ziva! Goes to Lime Hollow's Fishing Festival

It was the woman's normal time to leave for work, so at first Ziva! felt no concern when the roof of her sleeping-hut opened. She raised her feminine pointy white nose for a treat.

To her utter astonishment, Ziva! felt herself being lifted out of her cozy bed and hugged tightly to her human's chest. "It'll be fun, my little love," she assured the tiny marsupial in her arms. "I've packed all kinds of treats, even a banana," she promised with a kiss. Then she slid Ziva! into her travel crate and latched the door.

Ziva! looked out through the crosshatch of bars. This was familiar; apparently they were going to Lucille's, or Marie's, or both. Both places were warm and quiet and calm, with snacks and smooches. Ziva burrowed down into the blue afghan until she was completely covered, and went to sleep.

An unusually long time later, she woke. Marie was there, getting into the car. Ziva! had never seen Marie outside of her home. And what in the world was the creature she had on her lap? Bigger than a possum but smaller than the dog at home, the little thing smelled like a baby, with an overlying sweet outdoorsy scent.

Ziva! put her nose to the holes in the side of her crate nearest Marie, and inhaled with short little snuffs, sounding like a small steam locomotive. She was very curious.

"Ziva!" Mom said, seeing her awake. "You've never seen a goat before. I've taken Aloysius out to the barn, but not you." She put her fingers inside the crate, and Ziva! grabbed hold with her hand, inspecting them interestedly with nose and tongue. Her human (and Marie and her baby goat) waited patiently for Ziva to satisfy her curiosity and let go.

They drove another short distance (compared to how far they'd come) and then down a steep, winding road, to come out on a woodsy clearing. Mom parked, and in a few minutes, pulled Ziva! from her crate.

It was overcast with a chilly wind, but her human was nice and warm and had her wrapped up in her arms. The little opossum clung tightly to Mom's braid and scarf, looking around. She didn't get to go outside very often, and it was fascinating.

In a few minutes, several other humans came by, some normal size and some very small. Mom crouched down so the small humans could pet Ziva! with their sticky little fingers. Ziva! promised herself a good long grooming when she got home.

Mom talked about how beneficial opossums are, their resistance to rabies, and made a point to ask the kids what would happen if an opossum got bit by a rattlesnake. "The possum would have a snack," the woman informed the kids. "Possums are immune to snake venom, and they love to eat snakes." This made even the adults seem more inclined to tolerate possums in their backyard.

After what seemed like an endless procession of small humans, some smelling deliciously of fresh fish, her human finally sat down with Ziva! on her lap, and produced the promised snacks. To the delight of a crowd of children, Ziva! stood upright to reach each grape and bite of cheese. As a final special treat, the woman peeled a banana halfway, and held it for Ziva!, who quickly grabbed hold of it with one strong hand, her fingers sinking deep into the soft fruit.

"Not with the little hand," Mom pleaded, far too late and not really meaning it anyway. Ziva! knew Mom loved when she used her hands, and that she didn't really mind a mess, at least not one made by an opossum (or any other critter, for that matter. The big dog made a sloppy mess every time he took a drink, and all Mom ever said was, "Shall we mop it up, or name it?")

Mom hugged and kissed Ziva!, allowing the young humans to see the love she felt for the little opossum, and how Ziva! clung tightly to her, returning that love.

Soon fewer and fewer people came by, until there were only a handful left, one of whom Ziva! remembered from the previous October's "Creatures of the Night" celebration. The nice man (Mom called him Glenn) gladly invited Ziva! onto his shoulder, letting her sniff his face and stand on his shoulder with her hands on his hat to check out the top of it.

Mom stood by and laughed, taking pictures, but Ziva! could tell from her voice that Mom wanted her back. Mom could only bear being deprived for so long, and two minutes was about her limit. She collected Ziva! from Glenn's shoulders and covered the little marsupial's face in kisses, promising to share the pictures later.

Mom was much better about sharing possum pictures than the actual opossums.

Sara

Chapter 1

The House Opossum

The small opossum pushed on through the snow, her eyes shut against the sleetstorm. She stumbled occasionally, weak from starvation and favoring her bitten left hind foot, only moving because she was too numb to stop. Her silver coat, once soft and warm, now stuck up in tufts on the sharply-defined ridges of her ribs and vertebrae, doing little to protect her from the icy wind.

Wearily she climbed another snowbank, only to slip and fall down the other side, landing on a salty-tasting gravel path cleared of snow. Large, loud, nasty-smelling machines whizzed past at impossible speeds, not two feet from the opossum's shivering form, but none stopped or even seemed aware of her in the darkness of the February evening. Hypothermia was quickly setting in, and the little possum could no longer summon the energy to continue. Head down, her frostbitten tail stretching limply behind her, she hunched there alone in the dirty slush, waiting to die.

She noted without caring that one of the big noisy things that went by turned around several yards ahead, headed back toward her, turned around again, and finally pulled over behind her and came to a halt. A door opened, and a human walked over to look down at her.

"I'm sorry, little possum," the woman said aloud. "I'll move you off the road at least. But first, are there any babies in your pouch?"

Suddenly the tiny marsupial felt herself hoisted up by her tail. Was this human about to kill her? Weakly she struggled, but about all she managed to do was twitch her back feet.

"Oh! You're alive!" the woman exclaimed, startled at the possum's movement. But instead of dropping her as the possum expected, the woman quickly carried her by the tail back to the car, laid her on a soft, warm seat, sat down beside her, and shut the door against the brutal cold. Gentle fingers touched the tiny possum here and there, and she lay very still. Soon the machine began moving again. Periodically the human talked to her in a soft, reassuring tone, as the small possum drifted in and out of consciousness.

She came almost awake when the woman picked her up to hug her against her chest (the car having stopped while she was asleep), and carry her tenderly into a house. The warmth of the house enveloped her in a welcoming embrace, and she was carefully laid on her side on a soft blanket. Hushed, hasty movements were punctuated by a machine beeping, then the possum felt her head being lifted, and smooth plastic slid between her teeth. Warm liquid, not quite water, soothed her parched mouth and throat. With great effort, she swallowed several times, earning praise from the woman, but she was too exhausted to show any interest in the liver the woman offered.

While picking the burdocks off her, the human found the three deep puncture wounds in her shoulder, and the hole in her swollen and painful foot, all infected, mementos of her encounter with a farm cat. At the time she'd felt lucky to get away alive, but the injuries had worsened instead of healing, sapping her strength at a time she could least afford it, and the bones of her foot had been crushed, leaving her unable to run or climb efficiently.

Vaguely she heard the woman say, "I doubt you'll live the night, but at least you won't die alone in the cold." Warm breath fanned her frostbitten ears. "I love you." That was the last thing the possum heard before she fell into a deep sleep, cradled close to the woman's heartbeat, her face pressed into the angle of the woman's neck and shoulder, wrapped in warmth and the feeling that her life mattered to this unlikely savior, *she* mattered.

Humans often underestimate the resilience of the hardy souls who survive in the wild. In the morning, the little opossum awoke feeling much better. Warm through and no longer dehydrated, she lifted her head and sniffed with interest at this strange environment, to the obvious surprise and delight of the human she already thought of as *hers*.

"Hey little love, you want some more Pedialyte?" the woman asked, steadying the tiny possum upright in her lap with one hand, while offering a small orange bowl with the other.

The little possum drank some more of the strange-tasting but pleasant not-water, then slurped down a bowl of warm liver. When she was done, she washed her face, then once again found herself held close in the woman's soothing embrace.

"I'm sorry I lifted you up by your tail," the woman apologized. "I had no idea you were even *alive*, much less what a sweet little person you are." Then the woman set the possum down on a flat square, and leaned over to peer closely. "Three pounds, one ounce," she read, her tone conveying worry. "You've got frostbitten ears, broken teeth, a cloudy eye, there's something terribly wrong with your foot, and your poor tail has frostbit vertebrae sticking out. Let's get you to the vet," she said, gathering the small opossum up in her arms again.

"Sara," she murmured into the possum's rough fur. "Your name is Sara," the woman announced, and Sara snuggled into her human's hug, gave a deep sigh, and went back to sleep, content.

After Sara had eaten another small meal, her human held her close for a long moment, then put her into a small cage.

"It's not a cage, it's a travel crate," the woman said, as if she could read Sara's mind. She lifted the crate and put Sara back in the car that had brought her to the warm house of love and good food, then the car started. Was she getting rid of her already?

After a few minutes' drive, the woman carried Sara's crate into a building that reeked of other animals, mostly cats and dogs, none of them happy. Trusting the woman despite instinct and experience, Sara allowed herself to be picked up and examined by a quiet man who was rather impolite, yet kind. She felt a brief sting between her shoulders, and was given a sweet pink liquid which she eagerly lapped up. Then she was allowed to go back in the travel crate, and to Sara's relief, she was taken back to the house she considered her new home.

After just a few days of this lavish new lifestyle, Sara had gained over a pound, and no longer spent most of her time sleeping. She soon discovered that if she wandered around knocking things over in the middle of the night, her human would get out of bed (oddly enough, she slept during the night), kiss her and hold her, and occasionally even warm up a bowl of liver for her. Best of all, when she stood up or put her hand on the woman's leg, the human understood that she wanted to be picked up and held. Sara loved being pressed close to the woman's chest, hearing her slow, even heartbeat and breathing, feeling warm arms encompass her protectively.

Early one morning, the travel crate was brought downstairs, and Sara knew something was up. Sure enough, her human held her close, kissing a flat white spot into the fur on top of her head, then put her in the crate, and took her back to the place with the smell of scared animals. There, the woman set Sara's crate in a cage (and this *was* a cage, with a cement floor and stainless-steel bars), and settled her in as comfortably as possible.

"I promise, I'll be back this afternoon and bring you home," she vowed, kissing Sara's head. "I love you." Then, to Sara's dismay, her human protector walked out the door, leaving Sara alone in a room with a yowling cat and a large dog who whined constantly under his breath.

In spite of her many misgivings, Sara remained calm, hoping against hope that all humans were as gentle as the one who had saved and then so abruptly abandoned her. She missed the woman's soft murmurs of love and reassurance, and the feel of being held in that solicitous embrace. But possums are practical, and Sara licked her fingers and washed her face, preparing herself for whatever was to come.

One of the assistants came and took Sara out of the cage, talking softly and holding her gently. Sara relaxed, and didn't object when a clear plastic cone was placed over her face. She had only a few moments to notice a strange smell, then she fell asleep.

When Sara woke, the first thing she noticed was that her teeth that had ached so terribly were gone, replaced by a much milder pain and some annoying pieces of plastic in her gum that she couldn't wipe away with her dextrous fingers. She then noticed that the end of her tail had stitches too, and the dead bone that had stuck out was gone. For awhile she drifted in and out of sleep, then she heard her human's voice! She had come back for her, just as she'd promised she would!

Eagerly Sara woke, and tried to stand, but she was very wobbly. Her human kissed her repeatedly, then tucked her into the travel crate and took her home. Later that night, cuddled in the woman's lap, Sara drowsily revelled in the attention and love lavished upon her. She grasped her human's hand, and licked it thoroughly, leaving lots of 'possum spit to show her own love.

Chapter 2

Sara and the Yankees Fan

Sara woke to her human sliding the side of her sleeping-burrow open, and lifting her out. Drowsily keeping hold of the afghan with two fingers, Sara inadvertently unmade her bed and dragged it out along with her, until she came awake enough to transfer her grip to a fistful of her human's hair, her other tiny hand clutching the woman's shirt. Downstairs they went; Mom needed help with dinner, and Sara was her marsupial supervisor of choice.

In the computer room, the woman leaned over and invited Sara to step down from her arms onto a chair. Sara glanced briefly over her shoulder at the proffered cold, unhugging furniture, and twisted back around decisively, clinging upside-down to Mom like a silver five-toed sloth. The woman chuckled, and straightened, pressing her nose into Sara's nape and hugging her close, her breath warm in Sara's fur. Sara gave a didelphic sigh of relief and relaxed.

The woman held her thus for a delightful long moment, then she slid her hand between Sara and herself, palm to Sara's chest, gently prying Sara off her and holding her securely over the chair, and Sara gave in. She stretched out her hands to step onto the soft afghan covering the chair (no more did rough stones or sharp sticks ever touch Sara's callused soles) and the woman set her back feet down carefully, her hand running the length of Sara's tail (mindful of the tender end); then Sara was on her own on the chair.

With a quick kiss, the woman disappeared into the kitchen, and Sara looked around. Not a foot away was the bookshelf, and the tiny opossum hadn't reached adulthood by hanging around within predator's reach near the ground. She climbed onto the chair arm, then up on top of the back of the chair; from there Sara scrambled onto the narrow shelf, knocking over a couple books and sending a stuffed toy opossum to the floor, plastic Yankees hat and all.

Peering down over the edge of the shelf at the toy, Sara heard Mom's stockingfooted steps approaching. She'd heard the ruckus and come running.

"Sara! Are you all right?" the woman asked, hastily scooping Sara up off the shelf as if snatching her from the brink of a crumbling cliff. Before Sara could get a decent grip on her, Mom set her back down on the chair, restored the toy to its place of pride in the middle of the shelf, balanced the baseball hat back on its head, and then kissed the top of Sara's head, picked up her chair, possum and all, and carried her out to the kitchen.

Distracting Sara with a grape, the woman proceeded to start making dinner, setting out bowls and pulling various containers from the fridge. Sara watched carefully. Often she was called upon to make critical decisions – for instance, here was another one.

"Hey Angel," her human leaned over to kiss Sara again. "Do you want pear for dessert tonight, or apple?" Mom held out a sample of each for Sara's inspection.

Politely Sara sniffed the apple, but the decision had been made from the moment she heard the word "pear." Sara loved pears. Passing over the bite-sized piece of apple, she sank her worn front teeth into the half-inch cube of pear, rearranged it just right in her mouth with her hand, and chewed the savory snack with typical possum concentration, her eyes glazing over with bliss as she smacked.

When she'd chewed it down to flavorless pulp and spit out the crescent-shaped wad, Sara looked up, sniffing hopefully. Perhaps she could cadge another taste? But no, Mom had moved back to the counter and was spooning out yogurt.

Sara looked over the edge of her chair at the floor, and decided to climb down. This comfortable camp chair had a seat like a hammock and convenient crossed aluminum bars beneath, perfect for a possum to hold as she went headfirst over the side. Sara proceeded slowly, her tail curling around in the afghan on the seat to steady herself (unintentionally bringing it with her), only to halt when she felt Mom's hands on either side of her ribcage.

"Where are you going, little angel?" Mom asked, lifting Sara up and hugging her close. Mom used any excuse to hug Sara, and Sara loved her for it. Sara got a good fistful of the loose skin of her human's neck with one hand, and entwined her other in the woman's shoulder-length brown hair. If either grip hurt, Mom made no mention of it. She just pressed Sara to her with infinite tenderness, kissed her head and neck, and breathed warm into Sara's rose-petal ear: "Mmm, I love you, Sara Angel."

Sara sighed in contentment and relaxed onto her side in her human's arms, licking Mom's big fingers.

"But I do have to finish dinners," Mom interrupted in an apologetic tone, and set Sara back down on the chair. She put a few small pieces of cheese in front of Sara, and went back to the food and dishes on the counter. "Wait a few minutes, and I'll take you in and hold you, okay?"

Sara knew a bribe when one was placed on the chair before her, but this wasn't just any cheese, it was Meunster cheese, and Sara sat right there as her human wanted, and ate the cubes one by one in the unhurried fashion of opossums. Then she balanced her weight back on her haunches like an overgrown squirrel, and proceeded to wash up after her snack. She licked her hands till they fairly dripped, then scrubbed them over her eyes and down her face, over and over, until her fur was damp and stuck up in places, and she was thoroughly clean.

About halfway through, her human glanced over and saw what Sara was doing. Hastily she went to her purse, pulled out her camera and took some pictures. Mom took pictures of everything. Finished with her post-prandial grooming, and bored with this obsession to document her every move for posterity, Sara yawned her opinion of the camera, wide-jawed and toothily. Ironically, Mom photographed that, too.

"You've got possum breath," Mom commented approvingly, putting the camera aside and kneeling in front of Sara's chair, so she could hold the little possum's head between her hands reverently. Before Sara had taken that nap at the vet's, Mom had acted worried every time she smelled Sara's breath. Now she enjoyed it with a distinct air of relief and satisfaction.

Noticing that Mom was close enough, Sara reached up to place the palm of her right hand flat against her human's shoulder, her fingers spread out like a star in entreaty. Very rarely was she denied this simple request, and now dinner preparations remained forgotten as Mom scooped Sara up and wrapped her arms around the six-and-a-half pound opossum. Sara thrust her pointy white nose between Mom's shoulder and chin, making Mom chuckle as Sara's long whiskers tickled her face.

When her human had kissed her and settled her back onto her chair once more, Sara smacked her lips and sniffed the air. Was that cherry yogurt she smelled? She stared intently in the direction of the savory treat, sorting scents with the signature whispery whistle of her kind, until even a human could get the hint.

"You want your yogurt?" she asked, sliding a bowl beneath Sara's eager pink nose.

Gripping the rim of the bowl with both hands, Sara lapped at the semiliquid, squinting with pleasure at the sweet flavor. With each lap, some of the yogurt dripped back into the bowl from behind her inch-long fangs, but Sara kept lapping until her rough tongue scraped the bowl so clean it was dry. Then Sara proceeded to wash up all over again, this time including her ears, haunches and tail. A possum can never be too clean.

Chapter 3

Sara goes Geocaching at Lime Hollow

The small opossum knew she was going to have a sleepless day when her human got out the travel crate. Sure enough, Mom folded a blanket and placed it in the crate, then picked Sara up. Sara clung to the old blue shawl with tail and toenails, picking it up as Mom picked her up, only letting go when she got a good grip on Mom's shirt and hair. The woman kissed her head and shoulders, murmuring how much she loved having Sara with her when she visited her friends, then held her in front of the crate. Resigned, Sara walked in, feeling Sonia's ultra-soft afghan beneath her palms and soles.

Well, she felt the alpaca yarn with her hands and right foot, anyway. Sara's left foot was, as usual, covered in soft padding secured with snazzy purple vetrap. Ever since the farm cat had crunched down on her foot, sometimes when Sara put her foot down her toes folded under, and she inadvertently walked on the top of her knuckles. The sore spot had healed, but Mom still kept the protective bandages on. It felt odd, but didn't hurt, and Sara was getting used to it.

She was growing accustomed to going places, too. Even with the big fuzzy dog in the car with her, the movement and traffic noise, Sara just calmly dug into the blankets and slept until she felt the crate being brought out of the car.

The first place they went this morning was a farm, and Sara felt a twinge of anxiety. Farms have cats. Even inside the house, sure enough, Sara smelled cats, and didn't want to leave the safety of her crate. But Mom insisted, prying Sara's fingers from the bars of the crate door, and then all Sara could do was cling to Mom and hope her human had meant it, when she said she'd defend Sara to the last drop of her heart's blood.

Sara truly enjoyed how Mom held her close the entire time she was visiting, but Sara would far rather stay home and be held. However, no feral felines attacked, and when Mom offered her a piece of string cheese, Sara gently engulfed both the cheese and Mom's fingers in her wide mouth, worked the cheese loose, and chewed the luscious treat in trancelike pleasure. Mom gave her some water in an orange cup, and several more bites of mozzarella; tummy temporarily satisfied, Sara proceeded to wash her face and hands, generously spraying spit on Mom and the surrounding area.

Then with a contented sigh, Sara pressed herself close to her human, and went to sleep, vaguely aware of the occasional click of small wooden tiles on a cardboard surface, reassured by Mom's voice.

Then they went for another car trip, to Lucille's house. The dog accompanied them inside here, but Sara knew after that one experimental nip she'd taken on his foot weeks ago, that the big golden dog was afraid of her, so she ignored him. Here, too, there was food, this time scrambled egg from Mom's fork. It didn't take long for Sara to curl up in Mom's embrace, and relax into a semiconscious state. Really, didn't her human understand the concept of "nocturnal"?

Soon, they left that place too, and Sara rejoiced to be taken back to her home. But no, they weren't staying? Mom produced the baby sling, and tucked Sara inside; then they got in the car, and drove a short way. When the car stopped, Sara could smell grass and trees, birds and insects and other wildlife. This was unusual! She poked her sharp white snout beyond the edges of the baby sling, and sniffed with interest as Mom walked.

Wherever they were headed, it was a fairly long trip. Just as Sara was starting to get sick of the swinging of the pouch she was in, Mom hefted her up, baby sling and all, and held her up against her chest in the way Sara liked. Sara periodically peeked out at the woods and brush, but stayed in the circle of Mom's arms. She'd had enough of living in the wild, and kept both fists clenched tight in Mom's hair.

Finally they seemed to arrive at some sort of destination, although to the small opossum it looked like just another section of forest. To Sara's alarm, Mom pulled her partially out of the baby sling, despite Sara's desperate attempt to maintain a deathgrip on the woman's hair. Was she being dumped out here, to fend for herself again? Sara tried to climb inside her human's shirt, but she was easily overpowered, and soon found herself facing the woods, while her human fiddled with a metal box in front of her.

"I just want you to touch the geocache box with your little hand for a picture," Mom said, gently prying Sara's right hand loose.

Sara kept her face pressed to Mom's chest, and her hand balled into a fist. She felt the brief sensation of cold metal on her fingers, then Mom let her wriggle back into the warm dark bag. She wasn't being abandoned after all! Sara soothed herself by grooming, relieved to feel Mom start hiking back the way they'd come.

They got in the car, and soon Sara was home, grateful and glad to curl up, exhausted, in her camp chair. Mom tucked the blue shawl around her, and Sara fell asleep. She woke after some time, to find a piece of pear balanced on her fingers in front of her nose. She snatched it up and ate it, the schlurping sounds bringing Mom over, with more pear; then Sara went back to sleep. It had been a hard day.

Later she felt Mom re-doing the wrapping on her foot, and then Mom carried her into the bedroom, where she fed Sara a bowlful of cheese pieces by hand, ending with a scrumptious canned snail. After grooming herself and taking a big drink of water from the bowl on the nightstand, Sara felt much more alert – just as her human settled in bed with her.

Pleased to cuddle, Sara snuggled against Mom while she petted her, licking her own hands and Mom's until her human fell asleep. Then, fully awake (and noticing that the bed beneath her was damp with possum spit), Sara crawled out from beneath the flannel sheet, and sought out the pillow. Ahh, perfect for lick-rubbing! Gleefully Sara licked a layer of saliva onto the fuzzy fabric, then in ecstasy she dragged her face backwards in the spit, her eyes squinched half shut in pure pleasure. Over and over she repeated this, shoving her pliant human's head aside. She petted Sara drowsily and moved out of her way, and Sara continued until the pillow and her cheeks were soaked to her satisfaction.

Mom woke, briefly and incompletely, when Sara used the comforter and the bedframe to clamber down off the bed to the floor. Walking around the retriever stretched out by the foot of the bed, Sara hiked the length of the house to the stairs, then laboriously climbed up, hampered by the foot that would no longer grasp. She stopped for a drink from the bowl by the closet, then pushed under the bed and tucked herself into the ruffle and blanket at the corner, and went to sleep.

She woke to Mom stroking her fur. Without bothering to get up, Sara licked the fingers so much larger than her own, settled her chin comfortably on Mom's wet hand, and went back to sleep.

When she awoke some hours later, Mom was gone. Lonely and hungry, Sara awkwardly made her way headfirst down the stairs (which offered nothing for her tail to grasp to steady her descent.) Then she detoured behind the kitchen table, ambled through the computer room, bypassed the sleeping black-and-white dog, and stepped around the retriever twitching in his dreams in the bedroom.

Making her way beneath the bed to the corner between the nightstand, the wall and the bed, Sara pulled herself up against the side of the mattress, clutching at the sheets and scrabbling at the side of the wooden nightstand where Sonia slept, asking to be lifted up onto the bed.

After a few moments, Mom woke and tenderly scooped her up, scooching backward so Sara couldn't get into the nightstand with Sonia (Sara climbed Mom to check.) Mom produced a bowlful of pear which Sara made short work of, then some water, which Sara refused. Carefully she cleaned her sticky fingers, then put both hands on Mom's forearm, flopped over onto her side with her spine pressed against her human's stomach and her head in the crook of her elbow, and went to sleep, comfortable and content.

Chapter 4

Sara's Midnight Smooches

"Sara?" The small opossum woke to her human reaching beneath the bed and sliding both hands beneath her six-and-a-half-pound body, then gently pulling her out from her chosen cozy sleeping-spot. Sleepily Sara clutched at the woman's brown hair as she was carried down the stairs, feeling each step despite Mom's obvious attempt to walk smoothly.

The woman's arms around her slowed her heartrate back to normal, and when the woman kissed her on top of the head, Sara snuggled her white snout against Mom's neck contentedly. She gave a deep sigh and relaxed – just as her human stopped walking, and leaned over a chair with her.

"Want to help me with dinner?" the woman asked, bending low enough that if Sara let go, she could have reached out with one hand and touched the afghan folded neatly on the chair. Sara refused to let go.

Instead she clung tighter, thrusting her nose down the neckline of the woman's t-shirt, trying for a moment to wriggle into a pouch that wasn't there. Finally she remembered she was an adult, Mom wasn't really her mother, and treats and attention were lavished

114

upon her in this canvas chair. Assuming a royal air, Sara stepped down onto the soft blue afghan, sneezed, and washed her face.

As Mom often did, now she kneeled before Sara's chair, encircling the small possum with her arms, her head lowered to snuffle in Sara's fur, her breath warm and comforting. Sara circled the small space until her head was beneath her protector's chin; then she fell onto her side, sighed again, deeply, and went back to sleep.

When she woke, her human had left, draping a corner of the blanket over Sara. Mom loved tucking her in, and Sara loved feeling so cherished. Unfortunately, right now she also felt she had to pee. Reluctantly Sara worked her way out of the snug little nest, and shook her fur neat.

Mom was still nowhere to be seen, but Sara had been climbing out of trees long before she came to live in a human household; this chair hardly presented a challenge, even with Sara's handicapped foot. Over the side she went, working her way easily to the floor.

The big gold dog lifted his head in alarm as Sara approached his tail. Feeling benevolent, Sara elected to ignore him, and after she passed by, he laid his big head back down on the floor between his front paws.

"Sara!" Mom said, intercepting her. Happy to be held, and hoping to be taken to the bathroom, Sara twisted to face Mom and get a good grip on her hair and shirt. With a smooch, Mom asked, "What do you want, my special angel?"

Sara squirmed. She really had to go. Couldn't her human, so smart in so many ways, recognise such a basic need?

"Do you have to pee?" Mom finally asked, kissing the side of Sara's cheek. Sara sniffed the inside of her ear, making her chuckle, then Mom hustled her off to the bathtub.

Turning the sink faucet on, the woman turned and with infinite tenderness, carefully positioned Sara on her feet in the wet bathtub, then slowly removed her hands. "I know it's slippery, love," Mom murmured, letting Sara wrap her tail around her hand for support, as Sara's feet started to slide out from under her.

With an effort, Sara pulled her feet in as far as she could. Thirsty, she lapped at the beads of water clinging to the slightly-soapy slick surface under her fingers.

"No, no, no, love," Mom reproved, and an orange bowl of clean, fresh water appeared beneath Sara's nose. She lapped eagerly at it until it was about half gone, then she stepped resolutely around it, and squatted. Fortunately she was still on the thin side, and had a good three inches between her belly and the tub ("road clearance," Mom called it), so she only needed her hands and feet rinsed when she was done doing everything a possum could do.

"What a good possum!" the woman praised her, pouring lukewarm water into the tub so it ran over her fingers and toes on its way to the drain.

Knowing the routine, Sara stood up to balance on her back feet, weaving a bit on the insecure footing, her hands stretching up to reach for Mom, who quickly picked her up and set her on a thick, rich towel to dry her off before carrying her back to her chair.

"There, now we don't have to worry about getting your little pink bootie wet later," Mom said happily, producing a strip of purple vetrap and a small piece of gauze. She held Sara's half-numb injured left foot as gently if it were eggshells, but still it felt uncomfortable, and Sara tried to pull away.

"I'm sorry, my angel," Mom said. "But the sore on your knuckles is almost healed, this really is helping." Deftly the woman laid the gauze on top of Sara's foot, and wrapped it loosely to just above the second joint. Mom was afraid to make it too tight, preferring instead to go through the whole process two or three times a night.

Finishing up the wrap with a too-large human baby bootie, Mom fastened the velcro strip and let Sara have her foot back. Awkwardly Sara set it down, then kicked out behind her a couple of times, in a vain attempt to rid herself of the cumbersome thing, but for the time being it stayed put.

A bowl of shrimp distracted her for awhile, after which Sara washed up and napped for a bit. Then Mom, now in pajamas and smelling damply of soap, scooped her up again, and took Sara into the bedroom and settled on her side with Sara next to her, turned off the light and went to sleep.

Sara, however, was just waking up. She lick-rubbed Mom's pillow, then paced down to the foot of the bed and made to climb down. Mom woke and caught her before she hit the floor, kissed her, and went back to bed.

Sara padded to other side of the bed, and climbed the nightstand, trying to get back up. Only half-awake, Mom lifted her up. Sara walked down the bed and across her ankles, then started sliding down toward the floor again. Mom set her safely on the hardwood, then stumbled over the dog and went back to bed. This time Sara chose Sonia's side to beg to be picked up, which Mom did, with many kisses; she gave Sara a drink of water, and taking great care to barricade the much bigger possum's nightstand den from Sara's inquisitive nose, dropped back to sleep ... until Sara set out down the metal curlicue at the foot of the bed. Again.

Finally Mom got up, and carried Sara to the recliner. Tipping back to a comfortable position, Mom pulled up the comforter and cuddled the little possum, as if it were her own idea. Settling in, Sara groomed vigorously, soaking herself and Mom liberally with possum spit; then she gave Mom a loving lick-rub, laid her head on Mom's chest, and went to sleep.

Sara only came groggily aware in the morning, when Mom carried her upstairs and laid her gently on the thick afghan in the cupboard to continue her didelphic dreams.

Chapter 5

Sonia

Curled up in her cupboard nook upstairs, Sara could hear Mom sobbing downstairs. It was Friday morning, but Mom hadn't gone to work. For the last few days, Sara's human had been especially needy, clinging to Sara and weeping to her about the big opossum who lived in the bedroom. Sonia was very old (for an opossum) and seemed to be nearing the end of her life, despite the veterinarian's best efforts. So Mom turned to Sara for didelphic consolation, which Sara willingly provided. She loved being held and hugged.

Hearing Mom trudge her way upstairs, Sara stood up in the narrow, dark burrow and waited. Mom would need Sara's help getting dressed, as she did every morning. Fondly the small possum wondered how the woman had managed to function from day to day before her arrival.

"Sara?" Mom called tearfully, before opening the cupboard. "I need you, angel," she mumbled through tears, as she gathered Sara into her arms, unhooking one of Sara's nails that got caught on the woollen afghan. Mom stood, and simply held Sara close for a long moment, before moving to the other room and bending over the bed so Sara could step down onto the tan-and-black patterned counterpane.

Sara held onto Mom's shoulder-length hair and the top of her pajamas with all her marsupial might, hanging upside-down. Clinging like a limpet usually bought her an extra minute or so of hugging, but today it worked too well – Mom straightened with her, hugging her tightly, and started sobbing again.

"I love you Sara, and I love how you love to be held," she said, not making much sense, but Sara could clearly see that she was upset. All Sara could think to do was lick Mom's hand, sending silent love and support, and although humans are sometimes unable to understand the simplest things, Mom clearly took comfort from Sara's sympathy.

"You really are a special angel," Mom murmured into Sara's nape. "Oh, Sara, I'm so scared Sonia's going to leave us." Slowly the woman pried Sara off her and set her on the bed. She leaned over to hug and kiss Sara. Then she opened the closet, staring into its depths long enough that Sara decided to hike up to the top of the bed and lick-rub the pillow.

Collecting her choice of clothes for the day, Mom shut the closet, tucked Sara into the crook of her elbow, and moved to the room with the sugar gliders. She set Sara on the blue quilt covering this bed, cleaned the gliders' cage, then stood next to the bed to get dressed. Sara came over and put her hand on the woman's leg, gazing up in entreaty.

Never was a request to be picked up ignored or denied, no matter how often Sara asked, or what Mom might be doing. "Oh, Sara, I love you," Mom whispered, hugging the small possum to her, breathing deeply of Sara's scent as if memorizing it. "But I have to finish getting dressed, and go be with my La Sonia," she added, tears close to the surface. Putting Sara back on the bed, the woman poured a small pile of dried mealworms in front of her from the jar. Sara set to with the singleminded concentration of a possum enjoying every molecule of a tasty treat.

When Mom was dressed, gently she lifted Sara up, wrapping her arms around the small possum and burying her nose in the fur of Sara's shoulders for a few seconds; then she took Sara back to the cupboard, and gave her a couple pieces of dry cat food as a consolation for being left alone, while Mom went to sit with Sonia.

When Sara had first arrived in this possum haven, she'd been awed by the magnificent female possum who reigned supreme over the household. At fourteen pounds, Sonia was over three years old – practically unheard-of for a wild opossum. Sonia slept in the nightstand next to the bed at night, and Sara occasionally tried to climb in with her, and learn the secret to her sleek, sturdy body and enviable weapon of a tail. But Mom never quite let Sara get more than a few inches from Sonia's face, which was probably just as well.

By mid-afternoon, Sara knew that Sonia was in her last hours, and Mom wasn't taking it well. From her nook in the cupboard upstairs, Sara could hear her calling the vet, with tears just below the surface of her voice. Then, for the first time since Sara moved in, Mom left the house without coming to tell Sara she loved her. She just went out the door with Sonia, and Sara heard the car start up and drive away. Mom must be very upset indeed.

When she came back, Sonia wasn't with her, and Mom was a mess. She came up and pulled Sara out of the cupboard without a word, hugging her shakily as she carried Sara downstairs, crying and sniffing sloppily all over the soft, silvery fur that Sara spent so much time grooming. Sara didn't mind. She licked Mom's hands as Mom held her with infinite tenderness and love and heartbreak of loss. Her hands tasted of tears.

All evening long, Mom barely left Sara alone at all, except to hold the tiny baby possum, Lily. Lily was too young to understand the tragedy that had just occurred, but her exuberant personality was enough to help raise the spirits of the human. She lick-rubbed Mom repeatedly, salving her sorrow with possum spit.

Then, while making dinner, Mom unthinkingly thawed out too many shrimp, her mind not entirely focused on what she was doing. When she noticed she had, out of habit, made enough for Sonia as well, she started crying all over again, kneeling on the kitchen linoleum to hunch over Sara in her supervisor's chair. Sara wriggled further beneath Mom's wet face, happy to be needed and able to help.

Eventually Mom got herself and dinner together, although Sara noted that Mom didn't eat anything. Still, it soothed the woman greatly that Sara had a good appetite, and she thanked Sara repeatedly for eating and being healthy.

Later that night, as Mom lay in bed, Sara snuggled close, gripping her hand and lick-rubbing her until they both fell asleep.

Chapter 6

Sara Watches While Mom Sleeps

Sitting on her camp chair, Sara watched her human closely as she prepared dinner, following her movements as she went from refrigerator, to stove, to counter – Yes! Finally, here she came with something for Sara.

"How do you feel about blueberries, love?" Mom asked, holding one out to her. Sara sniffed it with academic curiosity, then turned her head. She'd been hoping for pear.

"Oh, come on, they're good," Mom cajoled, cutting the big blueberry in half, then offering it to her again. "Doesn't that smell yummy?"

Sara sniffed again, and decided to give it a try, if only to mollify her human. She chewed contemplatively, then spit out the skin. Definitely not as good as pear, or even plum. Sara sneezed, moved to balance her weight on her haunches (something of a challenge, perched atop several layers of soft afghan), and washed her face with dismissive finality. Sometimes she had to be blunt and obvious for Mom to understand.

Ah, the wonderful consistency of her human's inability to understand even the simplest of body language. Mom interrupted Sara's washup to offer another of the tasteless blueberries. With the patience of an angel, Sara stopped in mid-swipe, politely sniffed the proffered fruit, then pointedly resumed freshening up.

"Don't you like them?" Mom asked, kneeling down before Sara's chair to pet her. Well, not everyone could be as smart as a possum. Sara grasped Mom's fingers with her hand, and licked her lovingly, to make it clear that it was just the blueberries she didn't like. Then she raised her narrow white nose into the air, and inhaled. She could smell that there was a plum on the counter ...

"Okay, you can have plum instead," Mom murmured into the fur of Sara's shoulder, as if she'd suddenly thought of it herself. "I bet Lily will like the blueberries."

Sara watched with satisfaction and anticipation as Mom sliced and peeled half a plum and arranged it in one of the small blue bowls that were just the right size for possums, and unbreakable to boot. The little possum knew Mom wouldn't let her have it until long after she'd eaten her yogurt and entree – sometimes Mom even fell asleep before serving dessert, and Sara had to wait until morning! But Sara knew she'd eventually get to enjoy it, so she wiggled her nose under a fold of her mohair afghan, and settled in to drowsily finish supervising dinner.

When Mom was finished, she went upstairs with the gliders' dinner, then came back down, took Sara to pee, then carried Sara into the bedroom, her arms wrapped completely around the six-and-a-half-pound possum, reassuringly secure but rather as if Sara were as fragile as a dozen elderly eggs. "You're so tiny," the woman said softly into Sara's rose-petal ear, as she often did.

Leaning over, Mom pried Sara's hands off her shirt and hair, and gently set the possum on the counterpane. Sara hiked over to the nightstand, braced her hands on the edge, and drank from the bowl of water. Then she turned, considered climbing down into the nightstand burrow, but then decided to perch atop Mom's pillow instead.

With a smile, the woman laid down on the bed, and buried her face in the soft undercoat of Sara's flank. "Mmmm," she exhaled into Sara's fur. "I'm beat, Sara love."

Sara sniffed her caretaker's face, touching her own cold, wet nose to her human's warm, dry one; then she took a few experimental licks of the curly brown hair brushing up against her silky gray fur. What an interesting smell ... flowers? Curious, Sara opened her mouth wide and gently skimmed her teeth over Mom's scalp, closing her jaws on a few strands of hair at the end. She smacked her lips. What an intriguing taste!

Mom chuckled quietly, and reached up without opening her eyes to stroke Sara's fur. "I love you, my special angel," she murmured drowsily, and tucked her hand up to Sara's side.

Sara ran her fangs over Mom's skull again, this time adding spit and nibbling on the hair; then the small possum applied the scented saliva to her haunch in a series of short nibbles, working from top to bottom. Over and over she repeated the process, careful that her sharp fangs never woke the sleeping human who trusted her so completely. Long after her human's breathing slowed and deepened in sleep, Sara only stopped preening when they were both soaked, satisfied that when Mom woke the next morning, her hair would still be wet.

With typical possum cleanliness, Sara took a few minutes to wash her face and hands thoroughly; then she settled in for a nap, leaning against her human's face, enjoying the rhythmic cadence of warm breath in her fur. Not really awake, Mom curled her arm more closely around Sara. Sara briefly licked the hand so near to her nose, then she shifted slightly to flop over onto her side, her spine pressed against Mom's face.

Sara fell asleep like that, knowing she was loved, and loving in return.

Chapter 7

Sara Visits the Goat Barn

Once again, Mom brought Sara's travel crate down and set it on the floor next to Sara's chair. "Hey Angel, you wanna go to Marie's?"

Sara knew this meant being hugged and kissed almost constantly for two or three hours, instead of sleeping curled up in her quiet nightstand in the bedroom; but Sara enjoyed her highly demonstrative human's affection even more than the average opossum, and there was usually compensation of the edible variety.

Mom arranged Sara's soft mohair blanket, made expressly for her with love in every stitch, in on top of the old lap-robe already in the crate; then Mom gently slid one hand beneath Sara's chest, scooped up Sara's bottom with her other hand, and knelt to hold her in front of the open door of the crate.

Steadying herself with one strong hand firmly curled around the wire of the door, Sara poked her nose inside, decided all was well, and let go of the door to step inside. Once in, she turned around, and Mom ran a loving hand lightly down Sara's spine, carefully tucked her scarred tail in, and closed the door.

When they arrived at Marie's, instead of going directly into the house as they usually did, Mom pulled Sara out of her crate in the driveway, and clutching Sara to her chest, wandered out toward the barn with her camera. Halfway there she stopped, and gently set Sara on an old sundial surrounded by flowers. The copper felt cool to the small possum's hands and feet, and Sara breathed in the warm sunshiny air as Mom took pictures. Then she scooped Sara up again and continued on to the barn.

"Marie?" Mom called. A white goat with brown ears peered out at them from between the wooden slats of the fence.

"Out here," came the faint answer. Mom gave Sara's head a quick kiss, and they followed the sound of her friend's voice. Sara wiggled a bit, trying to look around over Mom's shoulder as they walked down a whitewashed passageway to a room filled with hay.

Sara raised her pointy white snout high, and inhaled a kaleidoscope of fascinating scents. Even a human could smell the rich summer scent of hay, the warm aroma of does and kids, and over everything the sharp, ripe smell of mature billygoat. But sifting through all that, the small possum also detected the damp, earthy scent of mice, and the dry, feathery smell of pigeons – both quite tasty, and easy prey for a possum who can climb rafters in the dark.

Of course, Sara still carried a shotgun pellet deep in the muscle of her right arm from an angry farmer's gun, so she wasn't in any hurry to go after more mice. Why had that farmer wanted to kill her for hunting rodents that ate and pooped in his grain? A possum as smart as Sara simply couldn't fathom the stunning stupidity of some humans. She clung more tightly to Mom with gratitude and love, mouthing her neck and shoulder.

Marie was in one stall with three small goats, and invited Mom in. "These two are still on a bottle," Marie explained, holding plastic bottles for the smallest goats to suckle. They wagged their tails and butted the bottles.

Mom wandered over to the corner and crouched down, sliding a hand between Sara and herself. Gently she set Sara down on the thick pile of fresh hay, making sure she had her footing before letting go, then she pulled out her camera.

At first Sara sat very still, unsure of this place, but Mom was less than a foot away.

"It's okay, Angel," she said softly, reassuringly. Slowly Sara walked a few feet along the cement wall, enjoying the slightly scratchy feel of hay on her palms and soles, tasting a few strands of timothy experimentally before spitting them out. Of course Mom was documenting every move she made, each picture punctuated with a bright flash of light, but Sara was used to that by now.

When she had been on the floor for nearly two minutes, the older kid glanced her way. Instantly Mom gathered Sara up and held her close, pouncing on this flimsy excuse to have Sara in her arms again. The stall floor had been interesting, but Sara preferred being wrapped in her human's embrace, and she twisted her head to lick Mom's hands to tell her so.

On the way back to Marie's house, Mom detoured through the small patch of pumpkins laid out in rows on the lawn. Setting Sara down on the flattened spot where one was missing, she stepped back, snapped a quick picture, then scooped Sara up again, and they went inside.

Marie's house smelled cozily of cooking and coal stove. Mom sat and, holding Sara securely in the crook of her arm, she spread Sara's soft blanket over her lap, and gently slid Sara down so she was standing on her thighs.

Thirsty, Sara sniffed around. Mom offered some dried fruit, which Sara cheerfully ate; then some cheese; finally, she produced a small orange dish of water, and Sara drank her fill. She sat and watched as Mom and Marie moved little wooden blocks around on a board between them, content to be held, until she noticed that she really had to go to the bathroom. With no way to communicate this need to her devoted but dimwitted human, Sara tried climbing up Mom's shirt, only to be kissed and gently set back on her lap. Mom was paying more attention to the Scrabble game than to Sara.

With sudden decision, Sara clambered right up onto the cardboard game, sending wooden tiles skittering in all directions. Maybe now Mom would notice she needed help!

But Mom just chuckled, saying the game was over anyway, snapping pictures as Sara took a few steps on the slick surface, not even trying to figure out why Sara would behave so uncharacteristically.

Giving up, Sara shifted her back feet forward and outward, and pooped.

"Oh, Sara! I'm so sorry, I didn't know you had to go," Mom apologized, immediately cleaning up with a Kleenex. She tenderly picked up the small possum, encircled her with both arms and covered her with kisses. "Mmm, I love you, Sara Angel," she breathed into Sara's silken black ear.

Sara snuggled her face close against Mom's neck, clinging with hands, feet and tail to this human who loved her so completely and unconditionally. With her nose tucked inside the neckline of Mom's t-shirt, Sara gave a deep sigh of utter contentment, and closed her eyes in bliss, her fingers wrapped in Mom's hair.

Chapter 8

Sara Scales the Closet Shelves

The small possum woke to the feel of warm fingers running gently from her head down her body to her left foot. "Hey Sara," Mom said softly. "Do you have to go to the bathroom?"

Delicately her human pulled the protective sock off Sara's foot, then slid her hands beneath Sara's body and hugged Sara tight to her chest, encircling the tiny marsupial completely within the comforting protection of her arms. Sara clung tightly to Mom's hair and blouse with her dextrous little hands, pressed her narrow white nose against Mom's neck, and gave a deep sigh of contentment as she was carried down the hall.

Of course, once they were in the bathroom Sara knew she had to let go, but when Mom leaned over the tub, Sara stuck like a burdock until Mom pried her off with a hand against her tummy.

Carefully Mom set her on the slick tub floor, not letting go until Sara had her feet beneath her. Her misshapen left foot was numb and clumsy, and all of her joints ached. Even her tail wasn't as supple as when she was a young possum.

But Sara didn't dwell on might-have-beens. She was warm although it was winter, well-fed without having to hunt, and safe for the first time in her life. Above all else, she was loved, and Sara cherished that feeling, returning it tenfold.

However, she did have to go pee. Sara yawned, shook her fur neat, rearranged her feet, and peed. After she finished and curtsied, Mom poured warm water so it ran over her hands and feet and tail. This felt weird, so Sara backed away from it. In doing so, her sensitive tail discovered a slight incline behind her at the back of the tub, so Sara continued to back up it as far as she could, feeling around with the end of her tail until it encountered an edge she could grip. Her tail might be scarred, but it was still strong enough to effectively winch her up backwards until she stood precariously on the four-inch-wide edge of the tub.

It was narrow and slippery, but Mom had been hovering the whole time, and quickly offered a hand. Sara closed both fists in Mom's shirt as Mom scooped Sara up off the narrow perch, kissed her, and folded the wet little marsupial close to her heart.

"You got out all by yourself! I am so proud of you!" she murmured into Sara's silken ear. Sara turned to lick the big fingers that tenderly cupped her head, and pressed her face into the crook of Mom's neck with a sigh.

Mom took her over to the camp chair, but once there, she simply stood and held Sara for several long moments, her eyes closed, her nose nuzzled into Sara's furry shoulder. Sara happily held on, soaking up love and offering her own, enjoying her human's embrace.

Finally Mom peeled Sara off and set her down gently on the soft aqua blanket Mom had knitted for her.

"Here, Angel, let's put your sock back on," Mom cajoled, bribing Sara with a grape.

Aware that Mom had an ulterior motive, Sara gracefully accepted the grape bribe anyway. Chewing every last drop of sweet yumminess from it, she let Mom slip an infant sock over her bad foot and wrap a strip of velcro around it snugly. She was rewarded with a second grape, after which she balanced back on her haunches and washed thoroughly, including her hands, hips, ears, face – and Mom's hands as well, which Mom put in front of her for just that purpose. Mom loved when Sara groomed her, and Sara gladly indulged her.

Only after Sara gave a happy sigh and relaxed onto her side did Mom pull her hands away, saying, "It's Shrimp Night, my special angel." Sara closed her eyes and waited patiently, confidently, for dinner to be delivered.

It wasn't long before Sara woke to a warm shrimp held in front of her nose. Drowsy and comfortable on her side, she carefully took only the shrimp and not fingers in her teeth, rearranged it in her mouth with her right hand, then chewed with her eyes squinched in bliss. Then Mom set a shallow black dish down in front of her, filled with cooked peeled shrimp and a dollop of cherry yogurt, and Sara stood up to give it her full attention.

Mom stoked her softly and kissed the top of her head, flattening the fur into a white circle. "It's new, just for you. Your very own special little bowl, for my special angel."

Sara grasped the edge of the bowl with one hand, and dove in with the appreciation of a connoisseur, taking her time to savor every lap of yogurt and every bite of shrimp, finishing up by scraping the bowl clean and dry with her raspy tongue.

Thirsty, Sara looked up at her human, trying to convey her need, but Mom as usual did't understand. Well, there were two water bowls downstairs, not counting the one on the nightstand.

With matter-of-fact resolution, the small opossum peered over the side of the camp chair, then extended one hand down to the top of the aluminum X of the frame. From there she made her way slowly but surely headfirst to the floor, her tail pulling the afghan halfway along with her, all to the unavoidable accompaniment of the camera flash. Mom loved to take pictures of her.

Disdaining the slimy metallic water in the dog's dish in the kitchen, Sara moved off stiffly toward the clean ceramic bowl in the bedroom closet.

Early on she had learned the secret of the closet – how if she gave it a sharp *boop* with her nose while simultaneously pulling the edge with her hand, the door could be made to fold in the middle, allowing entrance into a quiet, dark space unvisited by any other creature. At first Mom tried to keep her out, saying it was too full; but when Sara wouldn't give up, Mom capitulated, cleaned out one corner, and added a blanket and water bowl.

Deftly now Sara opened the door, climbed over the shoes, and lapped at the cool water in the corner. Mom had become distracted by Lily, the newly-arrived baby opossum, so Sara set about looking for a good place to nap.

The blanket on the floor of the closet was nice, but when she raised her pink nose, she saw that above her rose a series of shelves holding folded material, arranged as if with a possum in mind. Sara started up, scaling this impromptu ladder with difficulty but determination, losing her sock along the way. When she reached the top, she burrowed between the layers of a set of plaid flannel sheets, and drifted off to sleep.

Some time later, she heard Mom calling her. Sara poked her nose out of her cozy nest to see Mom stick her head in the closet and look around. "Sara?" Bending down, Mom picked up the sock with its velcro strip still attached, as Sara watched and waited for Mom to notice her and lift her down.

But humans rarely glance higher than their own eye level. Mom gave the closet floor a quick scan, then turned and knelt to look under the bed. "Sara? Sara, you want a grape?"

Mom had snacks? Sara wriggled out from under the sheets, but the prospect of climbing back down the shelving daunted her. She paced back and forth on the edge of the shelf until a pillowcase worked free and fell to the floor, alerting her human to her presence and predicament.

"Sara!" Mom said, coming over and stretching her arms up. Sara eagerly gripped Mom's fingers with her strong hands, but couldn't quite bring herself to let go of the sheets with her feet and tail. Mom lifted her down awkwardly until Sara could transfer her viselike grip to Mom's shirt and the soft skin of her neck. The sheets dragged off the shelf behind her to land in a heap on the floor with the pillowcase.

But Mom paid no attention to the mess. Kissing Sara soundly, Mom produced a freshly-rinsed grape, which Sara accepted. She had some difficulty trying to bite into the round, slippery fruit, but refused to let go of Mom with either hand. Eventually she got her teeth to bear and chewed blissfully, dripping sticky juice onto Mom's blouse. Mom didn't mind. She just chuckled into Sara's fur, and gave her another grape.

Basil

Chapter 1

Basil, Brownies and Lime Hollow

The smell of grapes woke Basil from the first tendrils of his daytime sleep. Drowsily he roused his eleven-pound didelphic self to pursue the piece of fruit, which his human held just out of his reach. Step by step she drew him out of his bed behind the bathtub. Uh-oh, Basil knew what that meant! She must want to take him with her and cuddle him.

A typically affectionate and demonstrative opossum, Basil enjoyed cuddling as much or more than the next person – but really, five hours of it sometimes seemed just a bit much. Still, he loved grapes. With a sigh he stepped out from around the corner of the tub and stood upright against her leg to accept the treat. Well aware that he was now dangerously within reach, Basil nonetheless took his time to chew the grape thoroughly, savoring every iota of sweetness before spitting out the bitter skin. Then, just as he'd expected, she scooped him up and kissed him, and stuffed him in his travel crate.

Resigned, Basil curled up to endure the jouncing of the Jeep ride.

When they stopped, it wasn't at Marie's farm with the cream puffs, nor Lucille's home where it was calm and quiet, but a parking lot filled to overflowing with young, hyperactive humans. Peering out from the relative safety of his crate, Basil eyed the busy, noisy children with some trepidation. Surely his human didn't mean to bring him out of his crate here!

To Basil's dismay, she conveyed his crate into a carpeted room (with, thankfully, only a small number of children present), and opened his crate door. Clinging to the blankets, Basil managed to hold out against her until she ceased trying to pull him out, and instead pulled the blanket beneath him out, Basil included.

"The Brownies want to see you, love," she said in an undertone to him.

Since she was so determined to display him, all Basil could do was cooperate. He took a deep breath and settled himself in her lap as a dozen children gathered closely around, all staring at him and pointing and chattering. Wasn't his human supposed to protect him from this sort of thing? Instead, she seemed to approve of these unknown younglings wiping their sticky fingers on the luxurious coat that Bail preened to perfection every evening upon awakening.

Fortunately, the small humans seemed consumed by innocent curiosity, rather than animosity. Basil's human answered their questions and, taking ruthless advantage of the pacifistic nature of opossums, even invited the children to touch his ears and tail, and feel the soles of his feet. It seemed to Basil that twenty-four little hands all reached for him at once.

This was even worse than his human servant on a really needy day! Summoning all his patience, Basil squinched his eyes shut and tried to pretend they weren't there.

"Oooh, isn't that cute, he's asleep!

Soon – but not nearly soon enough to suit Basil – the children started losing interest, and his human allowed him to scuttle back inside this crate, where Basil fastidiously licked himself clean as best he could. What an experience. He sincerely hoped that his human didn't intend to make a habit out of publicly displaying him to entertain children.

Two weeks later, Basil once again found himself at the center of a group of kids, quite literally: the children all sat in a circle around him and his human. This time, however, his human came better prepared to show off his limited repertoire of tricks – Basil smelled shrimp.

"Up, up," she said, dangling a shrimp tantalizingly close over his nose.

Swaying slightly with nothing to hold onto to balance himself, Basil pulled himself erect on his haunches and stretched his white nose upward, mouth open.

She dropped the shrimp between his dagger teeth, and Basil went back to all fours to chew every last bit of delightful flavor from the treat. Twice more she coaxed him upright for shrimp, then she held both of her hands out to him, fingers closed, palms down.

Basil knew this game. Poking his sensitive nose between the fingers of one hand, he detected the faint scent of grape. Too faint, he decided, and shifted to check out her other hand. There it was! Basil pushed his pointy snout in and extracted a fat, sweet grape. Opossum-like, he took his time savoring it, smacking appreciatively, until all that was left was the sour skin, which he spat out on the carpet.

Next she offered just one hand, palm up but with her fingers curled around the grape so he couldn't reach it without biting her: another game Basil knew well.

"Give me your hand," she said unnecessarily.

Humoring her weird whims as he always did, Basil gripped her index finger with his left hand, and she opened her loose fist so he could have the grape. She repeated this procedure several times, while around them the children sat in rapt enjoyment. Although this was a much larger crowd, Basil decided that these were better-behaved – at least they didn't insist on petting him *en masse*. He switched hands with the following grape, only because his human took inexplicable delight at his ambidexterity.

"See? He can use either hand," Mom announced as proudly as if she were somehow responsible for his cleverness. When the grapes were gone, she picked up a different container.

"Do you want to see how fast a possum can move?" she asked the room in general. A chorus of eager assent answered her.

Intrigued by the scent of live cockroaches, Basil raised his head and sniffed the air. He loved roaches, and only rarely did he smell them without getting to eat at least one.

As he'd expected, she soon set a roach down near him. Instantly Basil snatched it up and sank his teeth into its crunchy carapace, ignoring the varied vocal reactions of the crowd.

"Ewww!"

"Aw, wow, cool!"

"Look at him chew!"

"Yuck!"

"Can you give him another one?"

To Basil's disappointment (but not surprise) his human answered, "Not right now. These other two are for Lime Hollow to keep," she explained.

Too mellow to maintain even a mild negative emotion on a full belly, Basil braced his hips on the woman's crosslegged lap, and set about washing up after his meal, as polite opossums do.

Chapter 2

Basil Plays Scrabble

"Basil."

Sleepily the male opossum curled up tighter, his little hands fisted against his face in the comforting confines of his den behind the full-length mirror.

"Baaaasil," his human wheedled, in that particular tone of voice she used when she had a really yummy treat for him.

With a sigh fetched from the silky soles of his feet, Basil uncurled and poked his nose out, sniffing. Was the treat worth giving up a decent day's rest? Because Basil was well acquainted with her penchant for dragging him about with her. *The American Express Opossum,* he thought wryly to himself: *Don't leave home without him.*

Testing the air, Basil detected the savory scent of mozzarella cheese. The stakes were high indeed. Yawning wide as only a possum can yawn, slowly Basil picked his way out from amongst the soft blankets, following his nose until he stood out in the open and she let him have the treat. Basil chewed happily, blinking in the early morning light as he waited, certain she would pick him up when he was finished enjoying the bribe.

Sure enough, no sooner had he swallowed than she scooped him up in her arms and soundly smooched him.

"Mmmmm. I love you, Basil Paul," she murmured into his fur.

Basil yawned again.

Gently she set him down in front of his travel crate. Gracefully accepting the inevitable, Basil stepped inside and turned around to face out, giving his tail a few drowsy licks. Then an afghan shut out the rest of the world, and Basil felt the crate picked up, heard the door open and the big dog accompany them, and felt his box being secured in the passenger seat of the Jeep. Where to this time? he wondered, as he braced against the pitch and yaw of the antique vehicle.

When the Jeep finally came to a stop, Basil's keen nose detected a myriad of farm-related odors: chickens, geese, peacocks, cats, and pervading everything, the unmistakable miasma of a large number of goats – a familiar farm. Ah, so they were back at Marie's for their weekly smooch-the-possum morning marathon.

This routine was not without merit, however; Marie's kitchen specialty was cream puffs, and Basil thoroughly approved. His human, of course, wolfed down the larger portion of any goodies (even denying him the smallest taste of some things, such as chocolate candy), but she always let him share when Marie made cream puffs.

Every week, the two women spent hours laughing and laying little wooden tiles on a flat board, while Basil napped fitfully on his human's lap. Occasionally she got so involved in the game that he could sneak a few laps of her ultra-sweet tea from the mug by her knee.

He really wanted to get down and explore the house, but every time he slid from her lap, she caught him and smooched him in reproof. Basil tried climbing up onto her shoulders and walking down her back to the floor, but that didn't get him any farther.

Uttering another patented opossum sigh, Basil curled up, cleaned his hands and face, then settled into a light doze.

The sound of his name caught his attention.

"I got 'basil'!" his human crowed.

Well of course she had him; he was right here on her lap! Humans could be so dense sometimes. Basil was just drifting back to sleep when he heard Mom ask, "How much is 'basil' worth?"

Not twelve hours earlier, she had whispered into his rose-petal ear that he was priceless beyond comprehension; now she was asking her friend for an assessment? What did Marie know of the time Basil spent soothing his human, often well into the wee hours of the morning, time he might've spent running on his wheel or perambulating about the house?

"Four, five, six, seven ... on a double-word score, that's fourteen points," Marie answered.

Basil snorted in disbelief and rearranged himself, tucking his head farther in beneath his feet. From priceless he had been demoted to a mere fourteen points? He gave his tail another few short licks, squeezed his eyes shut and emitted a deep, pre-sleep sigh. He had just begun to nap again, when several small wooden squares rained down on him.

"I'm sorry, love," his human said, retrieving the pieces and kissing him – as if that made up for yet another intrusion on his much-interrupted dreams.

Finding himself awake and rather overwarm, Basil shifted to lay on his side, and with his tongue and lips he applied a layer of possum spit to his hands and feet and tail, using evaporation to cool off. Always a considerate opossum, he included his human's hand in the effort as well, coating her skin with a generous amount of saliva.

She chuckled and wiped her hand off on her jeans.

Now there's gratitude, Basil thought. Maybe she just didn't understand he was trying to help her. He gripped her big clumsy hand with his own much smaller and more dextrous one, and kindly gave her another application of didelphic drool.

"Mmm, I love when you lick me," she said softly into the salt-and-pepper fur of his neck, but Basil noted that she dried her hand off again, this time on her shirt.

He loved her, but he didn't harbor any illusions about her IQ. Maybe if the human species managed to survive a few million years (a fraction of the time opossums have walked the earth), they'd be able to grasp simple concepts like cooling by evaporation, but for now it was clearly hopeless. Basil snuggled against her stomach and went to sleep.

Donna Fritz; Aunt Gerry Caldwell

Aunt Gerry with Louise (used with permission)

Photo by Johns Creek Baptist Church

Aunt Gerry is a beloved member of her local church and several other organizations, and appreciates the warm welcome with which Louise was received by all.

Donna Fritz lives on a small lake in a cozy cottage with two opossums, two birds, one cat, and one five-foot kingsnake. She has state and USDA licenses for wildlife rehabilitation, possession for education, and falconry.

Printed in the United States
By Bookmasters